Betty Crocker

easy
italian

100 Recipes for the Way You Really Cook

WILEY

Wiley Publishing, Inc.

Published by Wiley Publishing, Inc., Hoboken, New Jersey

For general information on our other products and services or for technical support, please contact our Customer Care Department within the United States at (877) 762-2974, outside the United States at (317) 572-3993 or fax (317) 572-4002.

Wiley also publishes its books in a variety of electronic formats. Some content that appears in print may not be available in electronic books. For more information about Wiley products, visit our web site at www.wiley.com.

Library of Congress Cataloging-in-Publication Data
Betty crocker easy Italian : 100 recipes for the way you really cook.
    p. cm.
  Includes index.
  ISBN 978-1-4351-2575-9 (cloth)
  1. Cookery, Italian. I. Crocker, Betty. II. Title: Easy Italian
  TX723.B46973 2010
  641.5945--dc22

                2010013140

General Mills

Editorial Director:
Jeff Nowak

Publishing Manager:
Christine Gray

Editor:
Grace Wells

Recipe Development and Testing:
Betty Crocker Kitchens

Photography and Food Styling: General Mills
Photography Studios and Image Library

Wiley Publishing, Inc.

Publisher: Natalie Chapman

Associate Publisher: Jessica Goodman

Executive Editor: Anne Ficklen

Editor: Meaghan McDonnell

Production Manager: Mike Olivo

Production Editor: Abby Saul

Cover Design: Suzanne Sunwoo

Art Director: Tai Blanche

Layout: Indianapolis Composition Services

Manufacturing Manager: Tom Hyland

Printed in China
10 9 8 7 6 5 4 3 2 1

Cover photo: Penne with Spicy Sauce
(page 78)

Our Betty Crocker Kitchens seal guarantees success in your kitchen. Every recipe has been tested in America's Most Trusted Kitchens™ to meet our high standards of reliability, easy preparation and great taste.

Find more great ideas at *BettyCrocker*.com

Dear Friends,

Who doesn't love Italian food? With this great collection of recipes at hand, it's never been easier to bring the tastes of Italy into your home kitchen!

With chapters ranging from Snacks and Soups to Desserts, you will find a delicious recipe for any occasion. Crostini and Sautéed Olives make great appetizers for your next family gathering! And who doesn't like the warmth of hearty soups like Minestrone Soup and Pasta and Bean Soup on a cold winter day? Whether preparing a meal for company or a quick weeknight dinner, you'll keep turning to the chapter on Salads and Sides, featuring great dishes like Panzanella Salad and Asparagus with Parmesan.

Who thinks of Italian food without thinking of delicious pasta and aromatic sauces? Classic dishes like Fettuccine Alfredo and Stove Top Lasagna surely will become staples of your Italian culinary repertoire. And don't hesitate to try your hand at preparing main courses you often order in restaurants like Veal Saltimbocca and Chicken Piccata. Then finish off the meal with scrumptious desserts like Tiramisu and Almond Torte!

Italian cooking never seemed so easy!

Warmly,

Betty Crocker

contents

Buon Appetito!

Italians have been taking food seriously for more than two thousand years, and amazingly, most of the food eaten in Italy today remains roughly the same. Though the flavors and dishes may change from one region to the next, the love and appreciation of good food remains constant. Many people find the basic Italian diet—with its emphasis on olive oil; pasta, grains and risotto dishes; sensible portions; and only occasional desserts—to be one of the most healthful ways to eat.

Flavors of Italian Cooking

Many of the flavors associated with Italian cooking are familiar to us. During the first centuries after the discovery of the New World, several new foods were brought to Italy, among them herbs, vegetables and fruits.

The tomato, of course, has become something of a symbol for Italian cooking—sliced fresh with basil, cooked to make sauces or sun-dried for soups, pizza, pasta and long-term storage. The herbs most commonly used to enhance the flavor of the tomato are basil and oregano, often paired with garlic and onion. These two herbs are essential to many Italian sauces, particularly in southern Italy. In the north, olive oil and tomato sauces give way to butter and cream sauces with more subtle and exotic flavors.

The hills and plains around the Mediterranean are thick with small groves of picturesque gnarled olive trees. A popular olive used in Italy for both cooking and pure eating pleasure is the Kalamata (or Calamata) olive. These plump, purplish black Greek olives are the easiest to find, and their flavor is powerful yet balanced. Two other olives often found are the large green Greek olive, Ionian, and from France, Niçoise olives. The Niçoise is small in stature but has a pungent taste; its color ranges from gray green to charcoal. Olives usually are sold with their pits, for the increased flavor. Large crocks of olives in various colors and sizes, in brine or flavorful marinades, are plentiful in the markets and shops throughout Italy.

Herbs are the hallmarks of Italian culinary identity, giving a world of unique taste sensations and flavor combinations. Due to the favorable climate, most commonly used herbs are found fresh at the local markets in the regions where they can be cultivated or gathered wild. The herbs described below appear most frequently in Italian recipes.

BASIL can be seen growing in small pots on Italian balconies. It is a sweet, aromatic herb that can be a flavor powerhouse. It is the preferred herb for tomato recipes and is a flavorful addition when tossed with fresh greens in a salad. It should be torn into pieces rather than cut because the cut edges darken quickly and some claim the flavor is altered.

BAY LEAVES are pungent and aromatic. Dried leaves are the most widely used form; however, Italians often use fresh bay leaves. The assertive flavor goes well with grilled meats, soups and stews.

MARJORAM is moderately aromatic with a slightly bitter undertone and is closely related to oregano. It can be added to most meat dishes, soups and vegetables and to robust salad dressings. It is used both fresh and in dried form.

MINT has a distinctive sweet aroma and flavor and a cool aftertaste. Wild mint is used in Roman cooking, and in Naples, mint is used with fried eggplant and zucchini.

OREGANO is strong and aromatic with a pleasantly bitter undertone. It grows wild everywhere in the countryside close to the sea. It is the most popular herb that is used dried.

PARSLEY is by far the most popular herb in Italian cooking. It is available in two forms, curly leaf and flat leaf. The flat-leaf variety, also known as Italian parsley, is widely used. In fact, Italians assume everyone uses the flat-leaf parsley, which is more strongly flavored, so they don't specify it in recipes.

ROSEMARY is a perennial bush whose leaves resemble pine needles. It grows wild near the sea and its name, in fact, means "sea dew." More popular in northern and central Italy than it is in the south, rosemary has a fresh, sweet flavor that can be very strong.

SAGE is an aromatic and slightly bitter herb used widely in the north. It is well suited for bread and meat stuffings, poultry, sausages and soups.

TARRAGON is known for its distinctive, slightly sweet aniselike flavor. It should be used with care because its strong flavor can easily overpower other flavors.

THYME is aromatic and pungent; a little goes a long way. It is excellent with poultry, fish, seafood, bread and meat stuffings and tomatoes.

The Italian Market

Many Italians still shop daily at small specialty shops, which are peppered throughout the neighborhoods in cities, as well as in small towns and villages. The Italian passion for food is reflected in the desire to use only the freshest and best seasonal ingredients. A daily shopping trip could start with a stop at the butcher or seafood shop to select the fresh catch of the day for a main course. Then on to the *frutta e verdure* where beautiful displays of fresh seasonal vegetables, fruits, and herbs resemble still-life oil paintings. At the bread shop, or *panetteria,* the shelves and display cases are brimming with golden-crusted local breads and rolls baked fresh that day.

Traditional open-air markets are also very popular. On certain days, traveling vendors set up stalls or park refrigerated trucks in a piazza or on city streets to proudly display their wares. Not only is it a place to plan the family meals based on what is available, it is also a place to share greetings and news with friends and neighbors alike.

Shopping trips to the market may not be part of your daily schedule. For that reason, you may want to keep these items in your "Italian pantry" so you can prepare a tasty Italian recipe any day of the week. For some recipes, a quick stop at the market to pick up a few fresh ingredients may be all you need.

Your Italian Pantry

Anchovy fillets in oil (canned)

Anchovy paste

Artichoke hearts, marinated and plain

Beans, lentils and split peas, dried

Bread crumbs, Italian-style dry

Capers

Cheeses (Asiago, Gorgonzola, mozzarella, Parmesan, provolone, Romano)

Chicken broth

Cornmeal, yellow

Crushed red pepper

Flour (bread, semolina)

Garlic

Herbs, dried (basil, bay leaves, dill weed, marjoram, mint, oregano, rosemary, sage, tarragon)

Honey

Instant espresso coffee granules

Mushrooms, marinated

Mustard (Dijon, stone-ground)

Nuts (almonds, hazelnuts, pine nuts, walnuts)

Olive oils

Olives (Kalamata, Gaeta, Greek green, pimiento-stuffed, pitted ripe)

Pasta, dried (various shapes and sizes)

Rice (Arborio), long-grain regular

Roasted red bell peppers, jarred

Spices (anise, cinnamon, nutmeg)

Tomatoes, Italian-style plum (Roma) and canned

Tomatoes, sun-dried

Vegetable broth

Vinegar (balsamic, red wine)

Wine (sparkling, red, white)

Sautéed Olives

Hot Artichoke Dip

Crostini

Spicy Meatballs

Artichoke-Basil Frittata

Filled Rice Fritters

Shrimp and Feta Pizza

White Bean and Spinach Pizza

Grilled Pesto-Chicken Sandwich

Egg Drop Soup Florentine

Tortellini Soup

Basil-Rice Soup

Minestrone

Chunky Tomato Soup

Lentil Soup

Spinach-Polenta Soup

Cream of Spinach Soup

Onion and Potato Soup

Pasta and Bean Soup

Homemade Beef and Vegetable Soup

Clam Chowder

1

snacks and soups

Sautéed Olives

Prep Time: 20 min ▪ Start to Finish: 30 min ▪ 20 servings

2 tablespoons olive or vegetable oil
2 tablespoons chopped fresh parsley
1 medium green onion, chopped (1 tablespoon)
1 teaspoon crushed red pepper
2 cloves garlic, finely chopped
1 cup Kalamata olives (8 oz), drained, pitted
1 cup Greek green olives (8 oz), drained,pitted
1 cup Gaeta olives (8 oz), drained, pitted

1 In 10-inch skillet, heat oil over medium heat. Cook parsley, green onion, red pepper and garlic in oil about 4 minutes, stirring frequently, until garlic just begins to become golden brown.

2 Stir in olives. Cover and cook about 5 minutes, stirring occasionally, until olives are tender and skins begin to wrinkle. Serve warm or cold.

1 Serving: Calories 40 (Calories from Fat 35); Total Fat 4g (Saturated Fat 1g); Cholesterol 0mg; Sodium 420mg; Total Carbohydrates 1g (Dietary Fiber 0g); Protein 0g

Hot Artichoke Dip

Prep Time: 10 min ▪ Start to Finish: 35 min ▪ About 1½ cups dip

½ cup mayonnaise or salad dressing
½ cup grated Parmesan cheese
4 medium green onions, chopped (¼ cup)
1 can (14 oz) artichoke hearts, drained, coarsely chopped
Crackers or cocktail rye bread, if desired

1 Heat oven to 350°F. In small bowl, stir mayonnaise and cheese until well mixed. Stir in onions and artichoke hearts. Spoon into ungreased 1-quart casserole.

2 Cover and bake 20 to 25 minutes or until hot. Serve warm with crackers.

1 Tablespoon: Calories 50 (Calories from Fat 35); Total Fat 4g (Saturated Fat 1g); Cholesterol 5mg; Sodium 115mg; Total Carbohydrate. 2g (Dietary Fiber 1g); Protein 2g

To save time, mix ingredients in a microwavable casserole. Cover with plastic wrap, folding one edge or corner back ¼ inch to vent steam. Microwave on Medium-High for 4 to 5 minutes, stirring after 2 minutes, until hot.

Crostini

Prep Time: 10 min ▪ Start to Finish: 20 min ▪ 12 appetizers

6 slices hard-crusted Italian bread or 12 slices baguette, about $\frac{1}{2}$ inch thick

1 large tomato, chopped (1 cup)

3 tablespoons chopped fresh basil leaves

1 tablespoon capers

$\frac{1}{2}$ teaspoon salt

$\frac{1}{2}$ teaspoon pepper

$\frac{1}{4}$ cup extra-virgin olive oil

12 slices mozzarella cheese (about $\frac{3}{4}$ lb)

1 Heat oven to 375°F. If using Italian bread, cut each slice in half. Place bread on ungreased cookie sheet.

2 In small bowl, mix tomato, basil, capers, salt and pepper. Drizzle 1 teaspoon oil on each slice bread. Spoon half of the tomato mixture onto bread. Top each with cheese slice. Spoon remaining tomato mixture onto cheese.

3 Bake about 8 minutes or until hot and cheese is melted.

1 Appetizer: Calories 155 (Calories from Fat 90); Total Fat 10g (Saturated Fat 4g); Cholesterol 15mg; Sodium 330mg; Total Carbohydrate 7g (Dietary Fiber 0g); Protein 9g

Spicy Meatballs

Prep Time: 1 hr 5 min ▪ Start to Finish: 1 hr 5 min ▪ About 36 meatballs

1 lb lean ground beef
1 tablespoon grated Parmesan cheese
1 teaspoon dried oregano leaves
$1/2$ teaspoon dried basil leaves
$1/2$ teaspoon garlic salt
$1/2$ teaspoon pepper
1 egg
2 tablespoons fresh lemon juice
$1/4$ cup olive oil
1 clove garlic, finely chopped
1 red jalapeño chile, seeded and finely chopped
1 small onion, finely chopped ($1/4$ cup)
4 medium tomatoes, chopped (3 cups)*
1 tablespoon dry red wine, if desired

1 Mix beef, cheese, oregano, basil, garlic salt, pepper, egg and lemon juice. Shape mixture into 1-inch balls.

2 In 10-inch skillet, heat oil over medium-high heat. Cook garlic, chile and onion in oil about 5 minutes, stirring frequently, until onion is tender. Add meatballs. Cook, turning meatballs, until meatballs are brown.

3 Stir in tomatoes and wine; reduce heat. Cover and simmer 30 minutes, stirring occasionally.

*1 can (28 oz) Italian-style plum (Roma) tomatoes, well drained and chopped, can be substituted for the fresh tomatoes

1 Meatball: Calories 45 (Calories from Fat 25); Total Fat 3g (Saturated Fat 1g); Cholesterol 15mg; Sodium 25mg; Total Carbohydrate 1g (Dietary Fiber 0g); Protein 3g

Artichoke-Basil Frittata

Prep Time: 25 min ▪ Start to Finish: 25 min ▪ 6 servings

1 can (13 to 14¹/₂ oz) artichoke hearts, drained, or 1 package (9 oz) frozen
    artichoke hearts, thawed
1 tablespoon olive oil
¹/₂ cup chopped red onion
2 cloves garlic, finely chopped
2 tablespoons chopped fresh or 2 teaspoons dried basil leaves
1 tablespoon chopped fresh parsley
6 eggs
¹/₂ teaspoon salt
¹/₄ teaspoon pepper
2 tablespoons freshly grated Parmesan cheese

1 Cut artichoke hearts into quarters. In 10-inch ovenproof nonstick skillet, heat oil over medium heat (if not using nonstick skillet, increase oil to 2 tablespoons). Cook onion, garlic, basil and parsley in oil 3 minutes, stirring frequently, until onion is tender. Reduce heat to medium-low.

2 In small bowl, beat eggs, salt and pepper until blended. Pour over onion mixture. Arrange artichokes on top of egg mixture. Cover and cook 7 to 9 minutes or until eggs are set around edge and beginning to brown on bottom (egg mixture will be uncooked on top). Sprinkle with cheese.

3 Set oven control to broil. Broil frittata with top about 5 inches from heat about 3 minutes or until eggs are cooked on top and light golden brown. (Frittata will puff up during broiling but will collapse when removed from broiler.)

1 Serving: Calories 140 (Calories from Fat 70); Total Fat 8g (Saturated Fat 2g); Cholesterol 215mg; Sodium 480mg; Total Carbohydrate 9g (Dietary Fiber 4g); Protein 10g

The cooked egg under the artichoke pieces may turn light green due to the acid in the artichoke hearts. This will not affect the eating quality or flavor of the frittata.

Filled Rice Fritters

Prep Time: 1 hr ▪ Start to Finish: 1 hr 20 min ▪ About 48 fritters

5 cups chicken broth

2 cups uncooked Arborio rice

2 eggs, beaten

1/4 cup freshly grated Parmesan cheese

1 tablespoon butter or margarine, softened

48 cubes (1/2 inch) mozzarella cheese

1/4 cup 1/4-inch cubes prosciutto or fully cooked ham (about 2 oz)

1/4 cup 1/4-inch cubes mushrooms

1 cup Italian-style dry bread crumbs

Vegetable oil

1 In 3-quart saucepan, heat broth and rice to boiling; reduce heat. Cover and simmer about 20 minutes or until liquid is absorbed (do not lift cover or stir). Spread rice on ungreased cookie sheet; cool.

2 In small bowl, mix rice, eggs, Parmesan cheese and butter. Shape into 1½-inch balls. Press 1 cube mozzarella cheese, 1 cube prosciutto and 1 cube mushroom in center of each ball; reshape to cover cubes completely. Roll balls in bread crumbs to coat.

3 In deep fryer or Dutch oven, heat oil (2 inches) to 375°F. Fry 5 or 6 fritters at a time about 2 minutes or until deep golden brown; drain on paper towels.

1 Fritter: Calories 75 (Calories from Fat 25); Total Fat 3g (Saturated Fat 1g); Cholesterol 10mg; Sodium 160mg; Total Carbohydrate 9g (Dietary Fiber 0g); Protein 3g

When you break into these stuffed rice fritters, the melted cheese inside pulls into threads that look like telephone cords. That's how they got the name in Rome of *suppli al telefono*—telephone cord.

Shrimp and Feta Pizza

Prep Time: 10 min ■ Start to Finish: 25 min ■ 6 servings

1 package (14 oz) prebaked original Italian pizza crust (12 inch)
1 tablespoon olive or vegetable oil
1/2 lb uncooked deveined peeled medium shrimp, thawed if frozen,
    tail shells removed
1 clove garlic, finely chopped
2 cups shredded mozzarella cheese (8 oz)
1 can (2 1/4 oz) sliced ripe olives, drained
1 cup crumbled feta cheese (4 oz)
1 tablespoon chopped fresh or 1 teaspoon dried rosemary leaves

1 Heat oven to 400°F. Place pizza crust on ungreased cookie sheet.

2 In 10-inch nonstick skillet, heat oil over medium heat. Cook shrimp and garlic in oil about 3 minutes, stirring frequently, until shrimp are pink.

3 Sprinkle 1 cup of the mozzarella cheese over pizza crust. Top with shrimp, olives, remaining 1 cup mozzarella cheese and the feta cheese. Sprinkle with rosemary. Bake 12 to 15 minutes or until cheese is melted.

1 Serving: Calories 400 (Calories from Fat 170); Total Fat 19g (Saturated Fat 10g); Cholesterol 100mg; Sodium 890mg; Total Carbohydrate 32g (Dietary Fiber 2g); Protein 25g

Who says you need tomato sauces on pizza? This classy version features two kinds of cheese and succulent shrimp, and it's a mouthful!

White Bean and Spinach Pizza

Prep Time: 15 min ▪ Start to Finish: 25 min ▪ 8 servings

2 cups water
1/2 cup sun-dried tomato halves (not oil-packed)
1 can (15 to 16 oz) great northern or navy beans, drained, rinsed
2 medium cloves garlic, finely chopped
1 package (14 oz) prebaked original Italian pizza crust (12 inch)
1/4 teaspoon dried oregano leaves
1 cup firmly packed spinach leaves, shredded
1/2 cup shredded Colby–Monterey Jack cheese blend (2 oz)

1 Heat oven to 425°F. Heat water to boiling. In small bowl, pour enough boiling water over tomatoes to cover. Let stand 10 minutes; drain. Cut into thin strips; set aside.

2 In food processor, place beans and garlic. Cover; process until smooth.

3 Place pizza crust on ungreased cookie sheet. Spread beans over pizza crust. Sprinkle with oregano, tomatoes, spinach and cheese. Bake 8 to 10 minutes or until cheese is melted.

1 Serving: Calories 240 (Calories from Fat 50); Total Fat 6g (Saturated Fat 3g); Cholesterol 10mg; Sodium 370mg; Total Carbohydrate 36g (Dietary Fiber 4g); Protein 12g

In an extra bit of a hurry? Use a 7-ounce container of roasted garlic or regular hummus instead of processing the canned beans and garlic cloves in the food processor.

Grilled Pesto-Chicken Sandwich

Prep Time: 15 min ▪ Start to Finish: 1 hr 35 min ▪ 4 servings

$3/_4$ cup basil pesto
4 boneless skinless chicken breast (about $1^1/_4$ lb)
$1/_2$ teaspoon salt
4 crusty oval rolls, split
2 plum (Roma) tomatoes, cut lengthwise into $1/_4$-inch slices
8 to 12 large fresh basil leaves

1 Place chicken in shallow glass or plastic dish. Brush tops of chicken with $1/_4$ cup of the pesto; turn chicken. Brush with another $1/_4$ cup of the pesto; sprinkle with salt. Cover and refrigerate at least 1 hour but no longer than 24 hours.

2 Heat gas or charcoal grill. Grill chicken uncovered 4 to 6 inches from medium heat 15 to 20 minutes, turning once, until juice is clear when center of thickest part is cut (170°F).

3 Spread remaining $1/_4$ cup pesto over cut sides of rolls. Place chicken on bottom halves of rolls; top with tomatoes, basil and tops of rolls.

1 Serving: Calories 575 (Calories from Fat 340); Total Fat 38g (Saturated Fat 6g); Cholesterol 65mg; Sodium 970mg; Carbohydrate 30g (Dietary Fiber 2g); Protein 30g

Egg Drop Soup Florentine

Prep: 35 min ▪ Start to Finish: 35 min ▪ 6 servings

1 can (49$\frac{1}{2}$ oz) chicken broth (6 cups)
$\frac{1}{2}$ cup uncooked rosamarina or orzo pasta
2 eggs
1 teaspoon freshly grated nutmeg
$\frac{1}{2}$ teaspoon white pepper
$\frac{1}{3}$ cup all-purpose flour
$\frac{1}{2}$ cup freshly shredded or grated Parmesan cheese
1 tablespoon chopped fresh parsley

1 In 4-quart Dutch oven, heat broth to boiling. Stir in pasta; reduce heat to medium. Cook uncovered about 10 minutes or until pasta is tender.

2 In small bowl, beat eggs, nutmeg and white pepper with fork. Gradually stir in flour, beating until mixture is smooth. Slowly pour egg mixture into broth mixture, stirring constantly with whisk or fork to form shreds.

3 Cook uncovered 5 minutes, stirring occasionally. Top each serving with cheese and parsley.

1 Serving: Calories 160 (Calories from Fat 55); Total Fat 6g (Saturated Fat 3g); Cholesterol 75mg; Sodium 1220mg; Total Carbohydrate 15g (Dietary Fiber 1g); Protein 13g

Egg drop soup isn't found only in Asian cuisine. The Italian version was originally served when people were ill because it is so easy to digest. It is generally made with semolina flour or some type of small pasta, as in this version, and herbs. In Rome, fresh marjoram is used and lemon juice is combined with the egg-broth mixture.

Tortellini Soup

Prep Time: 55 min ▪ Start to Finish: 55 min ▪ 8 servings

3 tablespoons butter or margarine
2 cloves garlic, finely chopped
2 medium stalks celery, chopped (1 cup)
1 medium carrot, chopped ($^1/_2$ cup)
1 small onion, chopped ($^1/_4$ cup)
2 cartons (32 oz each) chicken broth (8 cups)
4 cups water
2 packages (9 oz each) dried cheese-filled tortellini
2 tablespoons chopped fresh parsley
$^1/_2$ teaspoon pepper
1 teaspoon freshly grated nutmeg
Freshly grated Parmesan cheese, if desired

1 In 6-quart Dutch oven, melt butter over medium-low heat. Stir in garlic, celery, carrot and onion. Cover and cook about 10 minutes, stirring occasionally, until onion is tender.

2 Stir in broth and water; heat to boiling. Stir in tortellini; reduce heat. Cover and simmer about 20 minutes, stirring occasionally, until tortellini is tender.

3 Stir in parsley, pepper and nutmeg. Cover and simmer 10 minutes. Serve with cheese.

1 Serving: Calories 175 (Calories from Fat 80); Total Fat 9g (Saturated Fat 5g); Cholesterol 65mg; Sodium 1110mg; Total Carbohydrate 15g (Dietary Fiber 1g); Protein 10g

Basil-Rice Soup

Prep Time: 50 min ▪ Start to Finish: 50 min ▪ 6 servings

2 tablespoons olive oil
2 cloves garlic, finely chopped
2 medium stalks celery, chopped (1 cup)
1 medium onion, chopped (½ cup)
1 medium carrot, chopped (½ cup)
¼ cup chopped fresh basil leaves
¾ cup uncooked regular long-grain rice
2 medium tomatoes, chopped (1½ cups)
1 carton (32 oz) chicken broth (4 cups)
1 cup water
1 teaspoon salt
¼ teaspoon pepper
¼ cup freshly grated or shredded Romano or
    Parmesan cheese

1 In 4-quart Dutch oven, heat oil over medium-low heat. Stir in garlic, celery, onion, carrot and basil. Cover and cook 10 minutes, stirring occasionally.

2 Stir in rice and tomatoes. Cook uncovered over medium heat 5 minutes, stirring occasionally. Stir in remaining ingredients except cheese.

3 Heat to boiling; reduce heat. Cover and simmer about 20 minutes or until rice is tender. Serve with cheese.

1 Serving: Calories 185 (Calories from Fat 65); Total Fat 7g (Saturated Fat 2g); Cholesterol 5mg; Sodium 1170mg; Total Carbohydrate 26g (Dietary Fiber 2g); Protein 7g

Minestrone

Prep Time: 55 min ▪ Start to Finish: 55 min ▪ 6 servings

2 tablespoons olive oil

2 cloves garlic, finely chopped

1 medium onion, coarsely chopped ($\frac{1}{2}$ cup)

1$\frac{1}{2}$ cups fresh lima beans or 1 box (10 oz) frozen lima beans,
    rinsed to separate

2 medium carrots, sliced (1 cup)

1 medium potato, peeled, cubed (1 cup)

1 small tomato, diced ($\frac{1}{2}$ cup)

$\frac{1}{2}$ cup chopped red or green cabbage

1 tablespoon chopped fresh parsley or 1 teaspoon parsley flakes

1 tablespoon chopped fresh or 1 teaspoon dried basil leaves

2 teaspoons chopped fresh or $\frac{1}{4}$ teaspoon dried dill weed

1 bay leaf

3 cans (14$\frac{1}{2}$ oz each) vegetable broth (5$\frac{1}{2}$ cups)

$\frac{1}{2}$ cup uncooked farfalle pasta or medium pasta shells

1 In 3-quart saucepan, heat oil over medium heat. Cook garlic and onion in oil about 5 minutes, stirring frequently, until onion is tender.

2 Stir lima beans and remaining ingredients except pasta into onion mixture. Heat to boiling; reduce heat. Cover and simmer 15 minutes.

3 Stir in pasta. Cover and simmer 10 to 15 minutes or until pasta is tender. Remove bay leaf.

1 Serving: Calories 165 (Calories from Fat 45); Fat 5g (Saturated 1g); Cholesterol 0mg; Sodium 940mg; Carbohydrate 29g (Dietary Fiber 5g); Protein 6g

Chunky Tomato Soup

Prep Time: 1 hr 20 min ▪ Start to Finish: 1 hr 20 min ▪ 8 servings

2 tablespoons olive oil

2 cloves garlic, finely chopped

2 medium stalks celery, coarsely chopped (1 cup)

2 medium carrots, coarsely chopped (1 cup)

2 cans (28 oz each) Italian-style plum (Roma) tomatoes, undrained

4 cups water

2 cans (14$\frac{1}{2}$ oz each) chicken broth (3$\frac{1}{2}$ cups)

2 tablespoons chopped fresh or 1 teaspoon dried basil leaves

$\frac{1}{2}$ teaspoon pepper

2 bay leaves

8 slices hard-crusted Italian or French bread, 1 inch thick, toasted

1 In 4-quart Dutch oven, heat oil over medium-high heat. Cook garlic, celery and carrots in oil 5 to 7 minutes, stirring frequently, until carrots are crisp-tender.

2 Stir in tomatoes, breaking up tomatoes coarsely. Stir in remaining ingredients except bread.

3 Heat to boiling; reduce heat. Cover and simmer 1 hour, stirring occasionally. Remove bay leaves.

4 Place 1 slice toast in each of 8 bowls. Ladle soup over toast.

1 Serving: Calories 140 (Calories from Fat 45); Total Fat 5g (Saturated Fat 1g); Cholesterol 0mg; Sodium 880mg; Total Carbohydrate 21g (Dietary Fiber 3g); Protein 6g

Lentil Soup

Prep Time: 1 hr 30 min ▪ Start to Finish: 1 hr 30 min ▪ 6 servings

2 tablespoons olive oil
2 cloves garlic, finely chopped
1 medium onion, finely chopped ($^1/_2$ cup)
1 bay leaf
$^1/_2$ cup diced prosciutto or fully cooked ham (about 4 oz)
$^1/_4$ cup diced Genoa salami (about 2 oz)
$1^1/_2$ cups dried lentils (12 oz), sorted and rinsed
$^1/_2$ teaspoon pepper
1 can (49$^1/_2$ oz) chicken broth (6 cups)

1 In 4-quart Dutch oven, heat oil over medium-high heat. Cook garlic, onion and bay leaf in oil about 5 minutes, stirring frequently, until onion is tender.

2 Stir in prosciutto and salami. Cook uncovered over medium heat 10 minutes, stirring frequently.

3 Stir in remaining ingredients. Heat to boiling; reduce heat. Cover and simmer about 1 hour, stirring occasionally, until lentils are tender. Remove bay leaf.

1 Serving: Calories 225 (Calories from Fat 90); Total Fat 10g (Saturated Fat 2g); Cholesterol 15mg; Sodium 1000mg; Total Carbohydrate 24g (Dietary Fiber 9g); Protein 19g

Spinach-Polenta Soup

Prep Time: 20 min ▪ Start to Finish: 20 min ▪ 8 servings

2 tablespoons olive oil

2 cloves garlic, finely chopped

1 medium onion, finely chopped ($^1/_2$ cup)

1 bag (16 oz) frozen cut-leaf or chopped spinach

3 cans ($14^1/_2$ oz each) ready-to-serve vegetable broth ($5^1/_2$ cups)

1 tablespoon freshly grated Parmesan cheese

1 tablespoon chopped fresh parsley or 1 teaspoon parsley flakes

$^1/_4$ teaspoon pepper

$^1/_2$ cup yellow cornmeal

1 In 3-quart saucepan, heat oil over medium heat. Cook garlic and onion in oil about 5 minutes, stirring occasionally, until onion is tender.

2 Stir in spinach and broth. Heat to boiling; reduce heat. Stir in remaining ingredients except cornmeal. Gradually stir in cornmeal.

3 Cover and simmer about 15 minutes, stirring frequently, until soup is slightly thickened.

1 Serving: Calories 90 (Calories from Fat 35); Total Fat 4g (Saturated Fat 1g); Cholesterol 0mg; Sodium 730mg; Total Carbohydrate 12g (Dietary Fiber 2g); Protein 3g

When adding the cornmeal, stir the soup constantly so the cornmeal won't clump together and make the soup grainy rather than thick and creamy. The cornmeal helps to thicken this hearty soup to just the right consistency.

Cream of Spinach Soup

Prep Time: 1 hr ▪ Start to Finish: 1 hr ▪ 6 servings

2 tablespoons olive oil
2 tablespoons butter or margarine
2 tablespoons chopped fresh parsley
4 cloves garlic, finely chopped
1 leek, thinly sliced
1 lb washed fresh spinach, torn into bite-size pieces
2 cups heavy whipping cream
2 cups milk
2 cups chicken broth
1 tablespoon fresh lemon juice
1 teaspoon freshly grated nutmeg
1 teaspoon salt
$\frac{1}{2}$ teaspoon white pepper
Additional freshly grated nutmeg, if desired

1 In 4-quart Dutch oven, heat oil and butter over medium-high heat. Cook parsley, garlic and leek in oil mixture about 5 minutes, stirring occasionally, until leek is tender.

2 Reduce heat to low; stir in spinach. Cook uncovered about 10 minutes, stirring frequently, until spinach is wilted. Stir in remaining ingredients.

3 Heat to boiling; reduce heat. Cover and simmer 30 minutes, stirring occasionally. Serve with additional freshly grated nutmeg.

1 Serving: Calories 385 (Calories from Fat 315); Total Fat 35g (Saturated Fat 20g); Cholesterol 105mg; Sodium 880mg; Total Carbohydrate 10g (Dietary Fiber 2g); Protein 8g

Onion and Potato Soup

Prep Time: 1 hr   Start to Finish: 1 hr   6 servings

3 tablespoons butter or margarine

2 large white onions, thinly sliced

2 tablespoons chopped fresh parsley or $1/2$ teaspoon parsley flakes

2 cloves garlic, finely chopped

2 bay leaves

$1/2$ cup diced prosciutto or fully cooked ham (about 4 oz)

1 carton (32 oz) chicken broth (4 cups)

3 cups water

$1/2$ teaspoon pepper

4 large baking potatoes, shredded (4 cups)

$1/4$ cup freshly grated or shredded Romano, Parmesan
     or Asiago cheese

1 In 4-quart Dutch oven, melt butter over medium-low heat. Stir in onions. Cover and cook about 10 minutes, stirring occasionally, until onions are tender.

2 Stir in parsley, garlic, bay leaves and prosciutto. Cook uncovered over high heat 5 minutes, stirring frequently. Stir in remaining ingredients except cheese.

3 Heat to boiling; reduce heat. Cover and simmer 30 minutes, stirring occasionally. Remove bay leaves. Serve with cheese.

1 Serving: Calories 230 (Calories from Fat 80); Total Fat 9g (Saturated Fat 5g); Cholesterol 25mg; Sodium 950mg; Total Carbohydrate 30g (Dietary Fiber 3g); Protein 10g

Pasta and Bean Soup

Prep Time: 2 hr 20 min ▌ Start to Finish: 3 hr 20 min ▌ 8 servings

$^1/_2$ cup dried lima beans

$^1/_2$ cup dried kidney beans

2 tablespoons olive oil

$^1/_2$ cup chopped lean bacon

2 cloves garlic, finely chopped

2 medium stalks celery, finely chopped (1 cup)

1 medium carrot, finely chopped ($^1/_2$ cup)

1 medium onion, finely chopped ($^1/_2$ cup)

$^1/_2$ cup dried split peas

1 can (49$^1/_2$ oz) chicken broth (6 cups)

2 cups water

1 teaspoon salt

$^1/_2$ teaspoon pepper

2 bay leaves

1 cup uncooked rigatoni pasta

1 In 2-quart saucepan, cover lima and kidney beans with cold water; heat to boiling. Boil 2 minutes; remove from heat. Cover and let stand 1 hour; drain.

2 In 6-quart Dutch oven, heat oil over medium heat. Cook bacon, garlic, celery, carrot and onion in oil 10 minutes, stirring occasionally. Stir in bean mixture and remaining ingredients except pasta.

3 Heat to boiling; reduce heat. Cover and simmer 1 hour 30 minutes, stirring occasionally, until beans are tender.

4 Heat to boiling. Stir in pasta; reduce heat. Cover and cook about 12 minutes or until pasta is tender. Remove bay leaves.

1 Serving: Calories 175 (Calories from Fat 25); Total Fat 3g (Saturated Fat 1g); Cholesterol 0mg; Sodium 1120mg; Total Carbohydrate 31g (Dietary Fiber 7g); Protein 13g

Homemade Beef and Vegetable Soup

Prep Time: 1 hr 30 min ▪ Start to Finish: 1 hr 30 min ▪ 8 servings

1 lb beef round, tip or chuck steak, about $3/4$ inch thick
1 tablespoon olive oil
1 clove garlic, finely chopped
1 medium onion, chopped ($1/2$ cup)
2 large romaine leaves, torn into bite-size pieces
2 large red cabbage leaves, coarsely chopped
2 medium stalks celery, chopped (1 cup)
1 medium potato, chopped (1 cup)
1 medium tomato, chopped ($3/4$ cup)
1 medium carrot, chopped ($1/2$ cup)
1 bay leaf
4 quarts water
$1/2$ cup dried split peas
1 tablespoon salt
$1/2$ teaspoon pepper
1 cup uncooked rotini pasta (3 oz)

1 Remove bone and excess fat from beef; set bone aside. Cut beef into 1-inch pieces.

2 In 6-quart Dutch oven, heat oil over medium-high heat. Cook beef, garlic and onion in oil about 15 minutes, stirring occasionally, until beef is brown.

3 Stir in bone and remaining ingredients except pasta. Heat to boiling; reduce heat. Cover and simmer about 45 minutes or until beef is tender.

4 Stir in pasta. Cover and simmer about 10 minutes or until pasta is tender. Remove bone and bay leaf before serving.

1 Serving: Calories 185 (Calories from Fat 35); Total Fat 4g (Saturated Fat 1g); Cholesterol 25mg; Sodium 920mg; Total Carbohydrate 25g (Dietary Fiber 4g); Protein 16g

Clam Chowder

Prep Time: 1 hr 15 min ▪ Start to Finish: 1 hr 15 min ▪ 6 servings

¼ cup olive oil
3 tablespoons chopped fresh parsley
4 cloves garlic, finely chopped
2 medium green onions, finely chopped (2 tablespoons)
1 small red Fresno or jalapeño chile, seeded, finely chopped
1 lb shucked fresh clams, drained, chopped
1 can (28 oz) Italian-style plum (Roma) tomatoes, drained
8 cups water
½ cup dry white wine or chicken broth
1½ teaspoons salt
½ teaspoon pepper
1 cup uncooked ditalini (short tubes) pasta

1 In 4-quart Dutch oven, heat oil over medium-high heat. Cook parsley, garlic, onions and chile in oil 3 minutes, stirring frequently. Stir in clams. Cover and cook 5 minutes.

2 Place tomatoes in food processor or blender. Cover and process until finely chopped. Stir tomatoes, water, wine, salt and pepper into clam mixture.

3 Heat to boiling; reduce heat. Cover and simmer 40 minutes, stirring occasionally. Stir in pasta. Cover and cook about 10 minutes or until pasta is tender.

1 Serving: Calories 220 (Calories from Fat 90); Total Fat 10g (Saturated 1g); Cholesterol 5mg; Sodium 800mg; Total Carbohydrate 28g (Dietary Fiber 3g); Protein 7g

Fresh Mozzarella and Tomato

Warm Tomato and Olive Salad

Panzanella Salad

Tomato and Potato Salad with Herbs

Warm Tricolor Bell Pepper Salad

Garlic and Romaine Salad

Fresh Basil and Spinach Salad

Marinated Rotini and Three-Cheese Salad

Bean and Tuna Salad

Marinated Mixed Vegetables

Sautéed Mushrooms

Savory Zucchini

Wilted Spinach

Brussels Sprouts with Prosciutto

Fresh Peas and Prosciutto

Asparagus with Parmesan

Stewed Garbanzo Beans with Onions

Eggplant Parmigiana

Cauliflower Au Gratin

Potatoes with Artichoke Hearts and Olives

Mashed Potatoes with Parmesan and Olive Oil

Pan-Roasted Potatoes

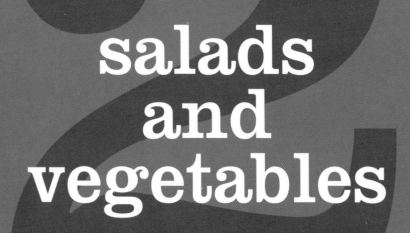

2

salads
and
vegetables

Fresh Mozzarella and Tomato

Prep Time: 10 min ■ Start to Finish: 40 min ■ 8 servings

4 medium tomatoes, cut into ¼-inch slices
8 oz fresh mozzarella cheese, cut into ¼-inch slices
2 tablespoons extra-virgin olive oil
2 tablespoons balsamic or red wine vinegar
2 tablespoons chopped fresh basil leaves
Freshly ground pepper

1 Arrange tomatoes and cheese slices alternately on round plate. Drizzle oil and vinegar over tomatoes and cheese. Sprinkle with basil and pepper.

2 Let stand at room temperature 30 minutes to blend flavors. Cover and refrigerate any remaining cheese and tomatoes.

1 Serving: Calories 115 (Calories from Fat 70); Total Fat 8g (Saturated Fat 4g); Cholesterol 15mg; Sodium 160mg; Total Carbohydrate 4g (Dietary Fiber 1g); Protein 8g

Warm Tomato and Olive Salad

Prep Time: 20 min ■ Start to Finish: 55 min ■ 6 servings

1 jar (10 oz) Kalamata olives, drained, pitted*
1 jar (10 oz) Greek green olives, drained, pitted
2 tablespoons olive oil
2 tablespoons chopped fresh parsley
2 cloves garlic, finely chopped
8 small tomatoes, cut into fourths
1/2 teaspoon salt
1/4 teaspoon pepper

1 Cover olives with cold water. Let stand 30 minutes; drain and pat dry.

2 Heat oil in 10-inch nonstick skillet over medium-high heat. Cook parsley and garlic in oil, stirring frequently, until garlic is soft.

3 Reduce heat to medium. Stir in olives. Cook uncovered 3 minutes, stirring frequently. Stir in tomatoes, salt and pepper. Cook about 2 minutes, stirring gently, until tomatoes are warm.

*1 can (5¾ oz) pitted ripe olives can be substituted for the Kalamata olives.

1 Serving: Calories 165 (Calories from Fat 135); Total Fat 15g (Saturated Fat 2g); Cholesterol 0mg; Sodium 1700mg; Total Carbohydrate 9g (Dietary Fiber 3g); Protein 2g

Panzanella Salad

Prep Time: 20 min ■ Start to Finish: 1 hr 20 min ■ 6 servings

4 cups 1-inch pieces day-old Italian or other firm-textured bread

2 medium tomatoes, cut into bite-size pieces

2 cloves garlic, finely chopped

1 medium green bell pepper, coarsely chopped

1/3 cup chopped fresh basil leaves

2 tablespoons chopped fresh parsley

1/3 cup extra-virgin olive oil

2 tablespoons red wine vinegar

1/2 teaspoon salt

1/8 teaspoon pepper

1 In glass or plastic bowl, mix bread, tomatoes, garlic, bell pepper, basil and parsley.

2 In tightly covered container, shake remaining ingredients. Pour over bread mixture; toss gently until bread is evenly coated. Cover and refrigerate at least 1 hour until bread is softened and flavors are blended but no longer than 8 hours. Toss before serving.

1 Serving: Calories 185 (Calories from Fat 115); Total Fat 13g (Saturated Fat 2g); Cholesterol 0mg; Sodium 340mg; Total Carbohydrate 16g (Dietary Fiber 2g); Protein 3g

Tomato and Potato Salad with Herbs

Prep Time: 45 min ■ Start to Finish: 3 hr ■ 6 servings

1 lb small red potatoes (about 8)
5 plum (Roma) tomatoes, cut into fourths
$^1/_2$ cup chopped fresh basil leaves
$^1/_3$ cup chopped fresh sage leaves
$^1/_3$ cup chopped fresh mint leaves
1 small onion, finely chopped ($^1/_4$ cup)
$^3/_4$ cup extra-virgin olive oil
$^1/_2$ cup red wine vinegar

1 In 2-quart saucepan, heat 1 inch salted water ($^1/_2$ teaspoon salt to 1 cup water) to boiling. Add potatoes. Heat to boiling; reduce heat. Cover and simmer about 20 minutes or until tender; drain. Cool until easy to handle, about 15 minutes.

2 Peel potatoes if desired; cut into $^1/_2$-inch slices. Gently toss potatoes, tomatoes, basil, sage, mint and onion. Pour oil and vinegar over potato mixture; toss gently until vegetables are evenly coated.

3 Cover and refrigerate at least 2 hours to blend flavors but no longer than 24 hours, stirring occasionally. Toss before serving.

1 Serving: Calories 230 (Calories from Fat 110); Total Fat 18g (Saturated Fat 3g); Cholesterol 0mg; Sodium 10mg; Total Carbohydrate 17g (Dietary Fiber 2g); Protein 2g

Warm Tricolor Bell Pepper Salad

Prep Time: 25 min ▪ Start to Finish: 45 min ▪ 4 servings

1/2 cup olive oil

2 cloves garlic, finely chopped

1 medium red onion, chopped

2 medium red bell peppers, cut into 1/2-inch strips

2 medium green bell peppers, cut into 1/2-inch strips

2 medium yellow bell peppers, cut into 1/2-inch strips

6 plum (Roma) tomatoes, peeled if desired, chopped*

1/2 teaspoon salt

1/4 teaspoon pepper

1 In 12-inch skillet, heat oil over medium-high heat. Cook garlic and onion in oil, stirring frequently, until onion is tender. Reduce heat to medium-low. Stir in bell peppers. Cover and cook about 10 minutes or until bell peppers are tender. Remove peppers with slotted spoon; set aside.

2 Stir tomatoes, salt and pepper into skillet. Cook uncovered about 5 minutes, stirring gently and frequently, until hot.

3 Remove skin from peppers if desired. Arrange peppers in star shape on large plate. Spoon tomatoes in center of peppers; pour liquid from skillet over top. Serve hot or at room temperature.

*6 canned Italian-style plum (Roma) tomatoes can be substituted for the fresh tomatoes.

1 Serving: Calories 320 (Calories from Fat 250); Total Fat 28g (Saturated Fat 4g); Cholesterol 0mg; Sodium 310mg; Total Carbohydrate 18g (Dietary Fiber 4g); Protein 3g

Garlic and Romaine Salad

Prep Time: 20 min ▪ Start to Finish: 20 min ▪ 8 servings

Salad
1 large bunch romaine, torn into bite-size pieces (10 cups)
1 small red onion, sliced, separated into rings
1 jar (6 oz) marinated artichoke hearts, undrained
1 cup Kalamata olives, pitted, or jumbo ripe olives
$1/2$ cup seasoned croutons
$1/3$ cup freshly shredded Parmesan cheese

Lemon Vinaigrette
$1/4$ cup fresh lemon juice
2 tablespoons extra-virgin olive oil
$1/4$ teaspoon salt
$1/4$ teaspoon pepper
2 cloves garlic, finely chopped

1 In tightly covered container, shake all dressing ingredients.

2 In large glass or plastic bowl, place romaine, onion, artichoke hearts and olives. Add vinaigrette; toss gently until evenly coated.

3 Sprinkle with croutons and cheese. Serve immediately.

1 Serving: Calories 100 (Calories from Fat 65); Fat 7g (Saturated Fat 2g); Cholesterol 5mg; Sodium 400mg; Total Carbohydrate 8g (Dietary Fiber 3g); Protein 4g

Fresh Basil and Spinach Salad

Prep Time: 20 min ▪ Start to Finish: 1 hr ▪ 4 servings

Salad
5 oz French or baby whole green beans or 1¼ cups 1-inch pieces
    regular green beans*
5 oz spinach, torn into bite-size pieces (3 cups)
5 oz fresh basil leaves, torn into bite-size pieces (3 cups)
2 hard-cooked eggs, coarsely chopped

Balsamic Vinaigrette
3 tablespoons extra-virgin olive oil
1 teaspoon balsamic vinegar
1 teaspoon fresh lemon juice
½ teaspoon salt
½ teaspoon freshly ground pepper

1 In 2-quart saucepan, heat 1 inch salted water (½ teaspoon salt to 1 cup water) to boiling. Add beans. Heat to boiling; reduce heat. Cover and simmer about 7 minutes or until beans are just tender; drain. Cool to room temperature, about 30 minutes.

2 In tightly covered container, shake all dressing ingredients.

3 In large glass or plastic bowl, place beans, spinach and basil. Add vinaigrette; toss until evenly coated. Add eggs; toss gently.

*1¼ cups frozen cut green beans can be substituted for the fresh green beans. Cook beans as directed on package; drain and cool to room temperature.

1 Serving: Calories 145 (Calories from Fat 115); Total Fat 13g (Saturated Fat 2g); Cholesterol 105mg; Sodium 350mg; Total Carbohydrate 5g (Dietary Fiber 3g); Protein 5g

Marinated Rotini and Three-Cheese Salad

Prep Time: 20 min ■ Start to Finish: 2 hr 20 min ■ 8 servings

Salad

1 package (16 oz) rotini or gemelli pasta
$1/2$ cup shredded mozzarella cheese (2 oz)
$1/2$ cup shredded provolone cheese (2 oz)
$1/4$ cup freshly grated Parmesan cheese
$1/4$ cup sliced pitted Kalamata or sliced ripe olives
$1/4$ cup sliced pimiento-stuffed olives
$1/2$ cup chopped pepperoni (3 oz)
$1/4$ lb salami, cut into $1/4$-inch pieces ($3/4$ cup)
1 small red onion, chopped

Fresh Dill Vinaigrette

$1/2$ cup extra-virgin olive oil
$1/4$ cup dry white wine or nonalcoholic white wine
1 teaspoon red wine vinegar
$1/2$ teaspoon salt
$1/2$ teaspoon sugar
$1/2$ teaspoon chopped fresh dill weed
$1/4$ teaspoon pepper

1 Cook and drain pasta as directed on package. Rinse with cold water; drain.

2 In tightly covered container, shake all dressing ingredients.

3 In large glass or plastic bowl, place pasta and remaining ingredients. Add vinaigrette; toss gently until evenly coated. Cover and refrigerate at least 2 hours to blend flavors but no longer than 24 hours. Toss before serving.

1 Serving: Calories 535 (Calories from Fat 280); Total Fat 31g (Saturated Fat 9g); Cholesterol 35mg; Sodium 1010mg; Total Carbohydrate 47g (Dietary Fiber 2g); Protein 19g

Bean and Tuna Salad

Prep Time: 25 min ▪ Start to Finish: 1 hr 25 min ▪ 6 servings

2 cans (15 to 16 oz each) cannellini or great northern
    beans, rinsed, drained
1 medium red onion, thinly sliced
1/3 cup extra-virgin olive oil
3 tablespoons red wine vinegar
1/2 teaspoon salt
1/8 teaspoon pepper
1 can (6 oz) tuna in water or oil, drained
2 tablespoons chopped fresh parsley

1 In shallow glass or plastic dish, place beans and onion. Shake oil, vinegar, salt and pepper in tightly covered container; pour over beans and onion. Cover and refrigerate at least 1 hour to blend flavors but no longer than 24 hours.

2 Spoon bean mixture onto serving platter, using slotted spoon; reserve marinade. Break tuna into chunks; arrange on bean mixture. Drizzle with reserved marinade. Sprinkle with parsley.

1 Serving: Calories 320 (Calories from Fat 115); Total Fat 13g (Saturated Fat 2g); Cholesterol 10mg; Sodium 300mg; Total Carbohydrate 38g (Dietary Fiber 9g); Protein 21g

Marinated Mixed Vegetables

Prep Time: 20 min ▪ Start to Finish: 2 hr 20 min ▪ 8 servings

2 cups broccoli florets (½ lb)
2 large bulbs fennel, cut into 1-inch pieces
4 oz mozzarella cheese, cut into ½-inch cubes
1 jar (10 oz) Kalamata olives, drained, pitted* (1¼ cups)
1 jar (8 oz) marinated mushrooms, drained
2 jars (6 oz each) marinated artichoke hearts, drained
½ cup extra-virgin olive oil
½ cup red wine vinegar
2 tablespoons fresh lemon juice

1 In shallow glass or plastic dish, place all ingredients except oil, vinegar and lemon juice. In tightly covered container, shake oil, vinegar and lemon juice. Pour over vegetable mixture; toss.

2 Cover and refrigerate at least 2 hours to blend flavors but no longer than 24 hours. Toss before serving.

*1 can (5¾ oz) pitted ripe olives can be substituted for the Kalamata olives.

1 Serving: Calories 265 (Calories from Fat 200); Total Fat 22g (Saturated Fat 4g); Cholesterol 5mg; Sodium 660mg; Total Carbohydrate 15g (Dietary Fiber 6g); Protein 8g

Sautéed Mushrooms

Prep Time: 15 min ■ Start to Finish: 25 min ■ 4 servings

2 tablespoons butter or margarine
2 tablespoons olive or vegetable oil
2 cloves garlic, finely chopped
$\frac{1}{2}$ teaspoon salt
$\frac{1}{4}$ teaspoon pepper
1 lb mushrooms, sliced (6 cups)
Chopped fresh parsley, if desired

1 In 12-inch skillet, heat all ingredients except mushrooms and parsley over medium-high heat until butter is melted. Stir in mushrooms.

2 Cook 4 to 6 minutes, stirring frequently, until mushrooms are light brown. Sprinkle with parsley.

1 Serving: Calories 140 (Calories From Fat 115); Total Fat 13g (Saturated Fat 5g); Cholesterol 15mg; Sodium 340mg; Total Carbohydrates 5g (Dietary Fiber 1g); Protein 3g

Lighter Sautéed Mushrooms: For 3 grams of fat and 55 calories per serving, omit oil and decrease butter to 1 tablespoon; use nonstick skillet.

Savory Zucchini

Prep Time: 15 min ■ Start to Finish: 30 min ■ 4 servings

1/4 teaspoon salt
2 tablespoons olive oil
2 anchovy fillets in oil, finely chopped
1 tablespoon chopped fresh parsley
1 tablespoon chopped fresh mint leaves
2 cloves garlic, finely chopped
2 medium green zucchini (1 lb), cut into 1/2-inch cubes
2 medium yellow summer squash (1 lb), cut into 1/2-inch cubes
1/4 teaspoon pepper

1 On large plate, place zucchini and summer squash. Sprinkle with salt. Let stand 10 minutes; pat dry with paper towels.

2 In 12-inch skillet, heat oil over medium heat. Stir in anchovies, parsley, mint and garlic. Cook 4 minutes, stirring frequently. Stir in zucchini, summer squash and pepper. Cover and cook about 8 minutes, stirring frequently, until zucchini is tender.

1 Serving: Calories 85 (Calories from Fat 65); Total Fat 7g (Saturated Fat 1g); Cholesterol 0mg; Sodium 220mg; Total Carbohydrate 4g (Dietary Fiber 1g); Protein 2g

To salt or not to salt, that is the question. In general, Italians buy their groceries daily, and the local produce is always fresh and in season. If squash is genuinely fresh, small and firm, skip the salting.

Wilted Spinach

Prep Time: 30 min ■ Start to Finish: 30 min ■ 4 servings

2 tablespoons olive or vegetable oil
1 medium onion, chopped (¹/₂ cup)
1 slice bacon, cut up
1 clove garlic, finely chopped
¹/₂ teaspoon salt
¹/₄ teaspoon pepper
¹/₄ teaspoon ground nutmeg
1 lb fresh spinach leaves
2 tablespoons lime juice

1 In 4-quart Dutch oven, heat oil over medium heat. Cook onion, bacon and garlic in oil 8 to 10 minutes, stirring occasionally, until bacon is crisp; reduce heat to low.

2 Stir in salt, pepper and nutmeg. Gradually add spinach. Toss just until spinach is wilted. Drizzle with lime juice.

1 Serving: Calories 115 (Calories Fat 70); Total Fat 8g (Saturated Fat 1g); Cholesterol 0mg; Sodium 410mg; Total Carbohydrate 7g (Dietary Fiber 3g); Protein 4g

Brussels Sprouts with Prosciutto

Prep Time: 35 min ■ Start to Finish: 35 min ■ 4 servings

1 lb Brussels sprouts
2 tablespoons butter or margarine
1/2 teaspoon chicken bouillon granules
1 small onion, thinly sliced
1/4 cup chopped prosciutto (about 2 oz)
2 tablespoons freshly grated or shredded Parmesan cheese

1 In 3-quart saucepan, heat 1 inch salted water (1/2 teaspoon salt to 1 cup water) to boiling. Add Brussels sprouts. Heat to boiling; reduce heat. Cover and simmer about 10 minutes or until tender; drain.

2 In 10-inch skillet, melt butter and bouillon granules over medium-high heat. Cook onion in butter about 5 minutes, stirring occasionally, until tender. Stir in Brussels sprouts and prosciutto; reduce heat to low. Cover and cook about 2 minutes or until hot. Sprinkle with cheese.

1 Serving: Calories 125 (Calories from Fat 70); Fat 8g (Saturated Fat 4g); Cholesterol 20mg; Sodium 380mg; Total Carbohydrate 11g (Dietary Fiber 5g); Protein 7g

Fresh Peas and Prosciutto

Prep Time: 40 min ▪ Start to Finish: 40 min ▪ 4 servings

1/4 cup olive oil
1/3 lb prosciutto, chopped (1/3 cup)
1 small onion, chopped (1/4 cup)
2 lb green peas, shelled*
1/2 cup chicken broth
1 tablespoon sugar
1 tablespoon chopped fresh parsley
1/4 teaspoon salt

1 In 10-inch skillet, heat oil over medium-high heat. Cook prosciutto and onion in oil, stirring frequently, until onion is tender.

2 Reduce heat to medium. Stir in remaining ingredients. Cover and cook about 10 minutes or until peas are tender.

*2½ cups frozen green peas can be substituted for the fresh green peas. Cover and cook 3 to 5 minutes or until peas are hot.

1 Serving: Calories 210 (Calories from Fat 135); Total Fat 15g (Saturated Fat 2g); Cholesterol 5mg; Sodium 520mg; Total Carbohydrate 16g (Dietary Fiber 5g); Protein 8g

Asparagus with Parmesan

Prep Time: 10 min ▪ Start to Finish: 20 min ▪ 4 servings

1½ lb asparagus
1 tablespoon olive oil
1 tablespoon butter or margarine
1 medium green onion, chopped (1 tablespoon)
1 clove garlic, finely chopped
½ teaspoon salt
¼ teaspoon freshly ground pepper
¼ cup freshly grated or shredded Parmesan cheese

1 Break off tough bottom ends of asparagus. In 3-quart saucepan, heat 1 inch salted water (½ teaspoon to 1 cup water) to boiling. Add asparagus. Heat to boiling; reduce heat. Simmer uncovered 4 minutes; drain.

2 Meanwhile, heat oven to 375°F. In ungreased 8-inch square pan, place oil, butter, onion and garlic. Heat uncovered in oven 5 minutes.

3 Spread asparagus in pan. Sprinkle with salt, pepper and cheese. Bake uncovered about 10 minutes or until cheese is melted.

1 Serving: Calories 100 (Calories from Fat 65); Total Fat 7g (Saturated Fat 3g); Cholesterol 10mg; Sodium 430mg; Total Carbohydrate 5g (Dietary Fiber 1g); Protein 5g

Stewed Garbanzo Beans with Onions

Prep Time: 15 min ■ Start to Finish: 3 hr 45 min ■ 6 servings

1 lb dried garbanzo beans (2$\frac{1}{3}$ cups)
3 tablespoons butter or margarine
8 slices bacon, cut into $\frac{1}{2}$-inch pieces
6 pearl onions, peeled, cut in half
2 cups chicken broth
$\frac{1}{2}$ teaspoon chopped fresh dill weed
$\frac{1}{2}$ teaspoon chopped fresh parsley
$\frac{1}{2}$ teaspoon pepper

1 In 3-quart saucepan, cover beans with water; heat to boiling. Boil uncovered 2 minutes; remove from heat. Cover and let stand 1 hour; drain.

2 In 10-inch skillet, melt butter over medium heat. Cook bacon and onions in butter, stirring frequently, until bacon is crisp. Stir in beans and remaining ingredients. Heat to boiling; reduce heat. Cover and simmer 2 hours to 2 hours 30 minutes or until beans are tender.

1 Serving: Calories 325 (Calories from Fat 125); Total Fat 14g (Saturated Fat 6g); Cholesterol 20mg; Sodium 440mg; Total Carbohydrate 44g (Dietary Fiber 12g); Protein 18g

Eggplant Parmigiana

Prep Time: 1 hr 5 min ▪ Start to Finish: 1 hr 40 min ▪ 6 servings

2 cups tomato sauce or tomato pasta sauce
2 small unpeeled eggplants (about 1 lb each), cut into 1/4-inch slices
1 egg
2 tablespoons water
2/3 cup dry bread crumbs
1/3 cup grated Parmesan cheese
1/4 cup olive or vegetable oil
2 cups shredded mozzarella cheese (8 oz)

1 Heat oven to 350°F. In shallow dish, mix egg and water. In another shallow dish, mix bread crumbs and Parmesan cheese. Dip eggplant into egg mixture, then coat with bread crumb mixture.

2 In 12-inch skillet, heat oil over medium heat. Cook half of the eggplant at a time in oil about 4 minutes, turning once, until light brown; drain on paper towels. Repeat with remaining eggplant, adding 1 or 2 tablespoons oil if necessary.

3 In ungreased 11 × 7-inch glass baking dish, place half of the eggplant, overlapping slices slightly. Spoon half of the sauce over eggplant. Sprinkle with 1 cup of the mozzarella cheese. Repeat with remaining eggplant, sauce and cheese.

4 Bake uncovered about 25 minutes or until sauce is bubbly and cheese is light brown.

1 Serving: Calories 410 (Calories from Fat 200); Total Fat 22g (Saturated Fat 7g); Cholesterol 60mg; Sodium 830mg; Total Carbohydrate 35g (Dietary Fiber 5g); Protein 17g

Cauliflower Au Gratin

Prep Time: 10 min ■ Start to Finish: 35 min ■ 5 servings

1 medium head cauliflower (2 lb)
1 medium red onion, cut into 8 wedges
1 tablespoon fresh lemon juice
1 tablespoon olive oil
2 large cloves garlic, finely chopped
1 tablespoon chopped fresh parsley
½ teaspoon coarsely ground pepper
2 tablespoons freshly grated or shredded Parmesan cheese
2 tablespoons freshly grated or shredded Asiago cheese
¼ cup shredded provolone cheese

1 Separate cauliflower into florets. In 3-quart saucepan, heat 1 inch salted water (½ teaspoon salt to 1 cup water) to boiling. Add cauliflower, onion and lemon juice. Cover and heat to boiling; reduce heat. Simmer about 6 minutes or until cauliflower is just tender; drain.

2 Heat oven to 425°F. Add oil to ungreased 9-inch square pan, stir in garlic and parsley. Heat uncovered in oven 5 minutes.

3 Spread cauliflower and onion in pan; sprinkle with pepper and cheeses. Bake uncovered about 20 minutes or until cheese is melted and forms a golden brown crust.

1 Serving: Calories 100 (Calories from Fat 55); Total Fat 6g (Saturated Fat 2g); Cholesterol 10mg; Sodium 160mg; Total Carbohydrate 9g (Dietary Fiber 3g); Protein 6g

Potatoes with Artichoke Hearts and Olives

Prep Time: 15 min ▪ Start to Finish: 40 min ▪ 4 servings

1 lb small red potatoes (about 8), cut in half
1/3 cup olive oil
1 small onion, thinly sliced
2 packages (9 oz each) frozen artichoke hearts, thawed, or 2 cans (14 oz each)
    artichoke hearts, drained
1/4 cup sliced pitted Greek green olives
2 tablespoons fresh lemon juice
1 tablespoon capers
1/2 teaspoon salt
1/8 teaspoon pepper
1/4 cup freshly grated or shredded imported Parmesan cheese, if desired

1 In 3-quart saucepan, heat 1 inch salted water (1/2 teaspoon salt to 1 cup water) to boiling. Add potatoes. Heat to boiling; reduce heat. Cover and simmer about 10 minutes or until tender; drain.

2 In 12-inch skillet, heat oil over medium-high heat. Cook onion in oil about 5 minutes, stirring frequently, until tender. Reduce heat to medium. Stir in potatoes and remaining ingredients except cheese. Cook uncovered about 5 minutes, stirring frequently, until hot. Sprinkle with cheese.

1 Serving: Calories 270 (Calories from Fat 135); Total Fat 15g (Saturated Fat 2g); Cholesterol 0mg; Sodium 930mg; Total Carbohydrate 36g (Dietary Fiber 9g); Protein 7g

Mashed Potatoes with Parmesan and Olive Oil

Prep Time: 10 min ■ Start to Finish: 35 min ■ 4 servings

6 medium baking potatoes (about 2 lb)
4 cloves garlic, peeled
$\frac{1}{2}$ cup extra-virgin olive oil
$\frac{1}{2}$ cup freshly grated Parmesan cheese
1 tablespoon fresh chopped parsley
1 teaspoon chopped fresh chives

1 Peel potatoes; cut into large pieces. In 3-quart saucepan, heat 1 inch salted water ($\frac{1}{2}$ teaspoon salt to 1 cup water) to boiling. Add potatoes and garlic. Cover and heat to boiling; reduce heat. Boil 20 to 25 minutes or until potatoes are tender; drain. Shake pan with potatoes gently over low heat to dry.

2 In medium bowl, mash potatoes and garlic until no lumps remain. Add remaining ingredients; beat vigorously until potatoes are light and fluffy.

1 Serving: Calories 435 (Calories from Fat 280); Total Fat 31g (Saturated Fat 6g); Cholesterol 10mg; Sodium 240mg; Total Carbohydrate 33g (Dietary Fiber 2g); Protein 8g

Here is a potato recipe that will turn a humble farmer's meal into a royal feast. Legend tells us that, while poor farmers could use only water and salt in their mashed potatoes, a young duchess in Parma loved this dish with extra-virgin olive oil and Parmesan; hence the nickname Patate della Duchessa Vergine.

Pan-Roasted Potatoes

Prep Time: 10 min ■ Start to Finish: 1 hr ■ 4 servings

6 medium baking potatoes (about 2 lb)
1 medium red onion, coarsely chopped
2 tablespoons chopped fresh rosemary leaves
4 cloves garlic, finely chopped
1/2 teaspoon salt
1/2 teaspoon pepper
1/4 cup olive oil
1/4 cup freshly grated or shredded Parmesan cheese

1 Heat oven to 375°F. Peel potatoes if desired; cut into 1½-inch pieces. In 13 × 9-inch pan, toss potatoes, onion, rosemary, garlic, salt and pepper. Drizzle with oil.

2 Bake uncovered 40 minutes, stirring occasionally. Sprinkle with cheese; toss until potatoes are evenly coated. Bake about 10 minutes longer or until potatoes are tender and golden brown.

1 Serving: Calories 350 (Calories from Fat 145); Total Fat 16g (Saturated Fat 3g); Cholesterol 5mg; Sodium 430mg; Total Carbohydrate 49g (Dietary Fiber 5g); Protein 7g

Angel Hair Pasta in Garlic Sauce

Vermicelli with Fresh Herbs

Fresh Tomato and Garlic Penne

Fettuccine with Wild Mushrooms

Tagliatelle Pasta with Asparagus and Gorgonzola Sauce

Spaghetti Puttanesca

Penne with Spicy Sauce

Mostaccioli with Vodka Sauce

Spaghetti Carbonara

Fettuccine Alfredo

Mediterranean Chicken with Rosemary Orzo

Chicken Tetrazzini

Chicken and Garlic Ravioli with Peppers and Sun-Dried Tomatoes

Spaghetti with White Clam Sauce

Bow-Ties with Salmon and Tarragon-Mustard Sauce

Parmesan Orzo and Meatballs

Bow-Tie Pasta with Beef and Tomatoes

Stove-Top Lasagna

Classic Meat Sauce

Classic Tomato Sauce

Tomato-Cream Sauce

Basil Pesto

Classic Risotto

Risotto with Shrimp

Three-Mushroom Risotto

3

pasta, sauces and risotto

Angel Hair Pasta in Garlic Sauce

Prep Time: 5 min ▪ Start to Finish: 20 min ▪ 6 servings

1 package (16 oz) angel hair (capellini) pasta
$^1/_4$ cup olive oil
$^1/_4$ cup chopped fresh parsley
4 cloves garlic, finely chopped
$^1/_2$ cup freshly grated or shredded Parmesan cheese
Freshly ground pepper

1 Cook and drain pasta as directed on package.

2 Meanwhile, in 12-inch skillet, heat oil over medium heat. Cook parsley and garlic in oil about 3 minutes, stirring frequently, until garlic is soft.

3 Add pasta to mixture in skillet; toss gently until pasta is evenly coated. Sprinkle with cheese. Serve with pepper.

1 Serving: Calories 410 (Calories from Fat 115); Total Fat 13g (Saturated Fat 3g); Cholesterol 5mg; Sodium 160mg; Total Carbohydrate 62g (Dietary Fiber 3g); Protein 14g

Vermicelli with Fresh Herbs

Prep Time: 20 min ▪ Start to Finish: 20 min ▪ 6 servings

1 package (16 oz) vermicelli
1 tablespoon capers
$1/4$ cup olive or vegetable oil
2 tablespoons chopped pine nuts
1 tablespoon chopped fresh parsley
2 teaspoons chopped fresh rosemary leaves
2 teaspoons chopped fresh sage leaves
1 teaspoon chopped fresh basil leaves
1 pint (2 cups) cherry tomatoes, cut into fourths
Freshly ground pepper, if desired

1 Cook and drain vermicelli as directed on package.

2 Meanwhile, coarsely chop capers if they are large. In medium bowl, mix capers and remaining ingredients except tomatoes and pepper. Stir in tomatoes.

3 In large bowl, toss vermicelli and herb mixture. Sprinkle with pepper.

1 Serving: Calories 390 (Calories from Fat 110); Total Fat 12g (Saturated Fat 2g); Cholesterol 0mg; Sodium 50mg; Total Carbohydrate 64g (Dietary Fiber 4g); Protein 11g

Fresh Tomato and Garlic Penne

Prep Time: 15 min ▪ Start to Finish: 25 min ▪ 4 servings

2½ cups uncooked penne pasta (about 8 oz)
1 tablespoon olive or vegetable oil
3 cloves garlic, finely chopped
12 medium plum (Roma) tomatoes (2 lb), coarsely chopped
2 tablespoons chopped fresh basil leaves
½ teaspoon salt
¼ teaspoon freshly ground pepper

1 Cook and drain pasta as directed on package.

2 Meanwhile, in 10-inch skillet, heat oil over medium-high heat. Cook garlic in oil 30 seconds, stirring frequently. Stir in tomatoes. Cook 5 to 8 minutes, stirring frequently, until tomatoes are soft and sauce is slightly thickened.

3 Stir in basil, salt and pepper. Cook 1 minute. Serve sauce over pasta.

1 Serving: Calories 290 (Calories from Fat 45); Total Fat 5g (Saturated Fat 1g); Cholesterol 0mg; Sodium 310mg; Total Carbohydrate 52g (Fiber 4g); Protein 9g

Fettuccine with Wild Mushrooms

Prep Time: 5 min ▪ Start to Finish: 1 hr ▪ 4 servings

1 cup hot water
1 package (about 1 oz) dried porcini (cèpe) mushrooms
8 oz uncooked fettuccine
2 tablespoons olive or vegetable oil
1 small onion, chopped ($^{1}/_{4}$ cup)
2 cloves garlic, finely chopped
1 cup heavy whipping cream
$^{1}/_{2}$ teaspoon salt
Coarsely ground pepper

1 In small bowl, pour water over mushrooms. Let stand 30 minutes; drain.*
Coarsely chop mushrooms. Cook and drain fettuccine as directed on package; keep warm.

2 Meanwhile, in 10-inch skillet, heat oil over medium heat. Cook mushrooms, onion and garlic in oil, stirring occasionally, until onion is tender. Stir in whipping cream and salt. Heat to boiling; reduce heat to low. Simmer uncovered 3 to 5 minutes, stirring occasionally, until slightly thickened.

3 Return fettuccine to saucepan. Pour sauce over fettuccine; toss until fettuccine is well coated. Serve with pepper.

*If desired, strain the mushroom soaking liquid and use in soups, stews or gravies.

1 Serving: Calories 445 (Calories from Fat 245); Total Fat 27g (Saturated Fat 13g); Cholesterol 115mg; Sodium 330mg; Total Carbohydrate 41g; (Dietary Fiber 2g); Protein 9g

Tagliatelle Pasta with Asparagus and Gorgonzola Sauce

Prep Time: 25 min ▪ Start to Finish: 25 min ▪ 4 servings

1 lb asparagus
8 oz uncooked tagliatelle pasta or fettucine
2 tablespoons olive or vegetable oil
4 medium green onions, sliced ($1/4$ cup)
$1/4$ cup chopped fresh parsley
1 clove garlic, finely chopped
1 cup crumbled Gorgonzola cheese (4 oz)
$1/2$ teaspoon freshly cracked pepper

1 Break off tough ends of asparagus as far down as stalks snap easily. Cut asparagus into 1-inch pieces. Cook pasta as directed on package, adding asparagus during last 5 minutes of cooking; drain.

2 Meanwhile, in 12-inch skillet, heat oil over medium-high heat. Cook onions, parsley and garlic in oil about 5 minutes, stirring occasionally, until onions are tender. Reduce heat to medium.

3 Add pasta, asparagus and cheese to mixture in skillet. Cook about 3 minutes, tossing gently, until cheese is melted and pasta is evenly coated. Sprinkle with pepper.

1 Serving: Calories 370 (Calories from Fat 160); Total Fat 17g (Saturated Fat 7g); Cholesterol 70mg; Sodium 640mg; Total Carbohydrate 40g (Dietary Fiber 3g); Protein 15g

Let your ingredients join forces! Adding vegetables to pasta water during the last minutes of cooking saves a major step (and saves you extra pans).

Spaghetti Puttanesca

Prep Time: 30 min ▪ Start to Finish: 30 min ▪ 6 servings

$^1/_3$ cup olive oil

2 cloves garlic, cut in half

1 tablespoon capers

4 flat anchovy fillets in oil, drained

2 cans (28 oz each) Italian-style pear-shaped (plum) tomatoes, drained and chopped

1 red jalapeño chile, seeded and finely chopped

$^1/_2$ cup sliced imported Kalamata or large ripe olives

1 package (16 oz) spaghetti

1 In large kettle or stockpot, heat oil over medium-high heat. Cook garlic in oil about 5 minutes, stirring frequently, until garlic just begins to turn golden. Remove garlic and discard.

2 Stir capers, anchovy fillets, tomatoes and chile into oil in Dutch oven. Heat to boiling; reduce heat. Simmer uncovered about 20 minutes or until slightly thickened. Stir in olives; keep warm.

3 Meanwhile, cook and drain spaghetti as directed on package. Add spaghetti to tomato mixture. Cook over high heat about 3 minutes, tossing gently, until spaghetti is evenly coated.

1 Serving: Calories 435 (Calories from Fat 135); Total Fat 15g (Saturated Fat 2g); Cholesterol 2mg; Sodium 430mg; Total Carbohydrate 68g (Dietary Fiber 5g); Protein 12g

Penne with Spicy Sauce

Prep Time: 10 min ▪ Start to Finish: 30 min ▪ 6 servings

1 package (16 oz) penne rigate pasta
1 can (28 oz) Italian-style plum (Roma) tomatoes, undrained
2 tablespoons olive oil
2 cloves garlic, finely chopped
1 teaspoon crushed red pepper
2 tablespoons chopped fresh parsley
1 tablespoon tomato paste
$1/2$ cup freshly grated or shredded Parmesan cheese

1 Cook and drain pasta as directed on package.

2 Meanwhile, place tomatoes with juice in food processor or blender. Cover and process until coarsely chopped; set aside.

3 In 12-inch skillet, heat oil over medium-high heat. Cook garlic, red pepper and parsley in oil about 5 minutes, stirring frequently, until garlic just begins to turn golden.

4 Stir in chopped tomatoes and tomato paste. Heat to boiling; reduce heat. Cover and simmer about 10 minutes, stirring occasionally, until slightly thickened.

5 Add pasta and ¼ cup of the cheese to mixture in skillet. Cook about 3 minutes, tossing gently, until pasta is evenly coated. Sprinkle with remaining ¼ cup cheese.

1 Serving: Calories 390 (Calories from Fat 80); Total Fat 9g (Saturated Fat 2g); Cholesterol 5mg; Sodium 380mg; Total Carbohydrate 66g (Dietary Fiber 4g); Protein 15g

Mostaccioli with Vodka Sauce

Prep Time: 20 min ▪ Start to Finish: 1 hr ▪ 6 main-course or 8 first-course servings

3 tablespoons butter or margarine

1 tablespoon olive oil

2 cloves garlic, finely chopped

1 small onion, chopped ($^1/_4$ cup)

$^1/_4$ cup chopped prosciutto or fully cooked ham (about 2 oz)

2 boneless, skinless chicken breasts (about $^1/_2$ lb), cut into 1-inch pieces

$^1/_2$ cup vodka or chicken broth

$^1/_2$ cup whipping (heavy) cream

$^1/_2$ cup sliced pitted Kalamata or large pitted ripe olives

1 tablespoon chopped fresh parsley

$^1/_2$ teaspoon pepper

1 package (16 oz) mostaccioli or penne rigate pasta

$^1/_4$ cup freshly grated or shredded Parmesan cheese

1 In 10-inch skillet, heat butter and oil over medium-high heat. Cook garlic and onion in butter mixture about 5 minutes, stirring occasionally, until onion is tender.

2 Stir in prosciutto and chicken. Cook about 5 minutes, stirring occasionally, until chicken is brown. Stir in vodka. Cook uncovered until liquid has evaporated.

3 Stir in whipping cream, olives, parsley and pepper. Heat to boiling; reduce heat. Simmer uncovered about 30 minutes, stirring frequently, until thickened.

4 Meanwhile, cook and drain pasta as directed on package. Add pasta to sauce; toss gently until pasta is evenly coated. Sprinkle with cheese.

1 Serving: Calories 530 (Calories from Fat 180); Total Fat 20g (Saturated Fat 9g); Cholesterol 70mg; Sodium 330mg; Total Carbohydrate 62g (Dietary Fiber 3g); Protein 23g

This is a modern pasta recipe popular in northern Italy. Cooks intrigued by different ways of cooking short-cut pastas found vodka to be an innovative addition to their repertoire. Brandy or grappa is sometimes substituted for the vodka.

Spaghetti Carbonara

Prep Time: 25 min ▪ Start to Finish: 25 min ▪ 6 servings

1 package (16 oz) spaghetti
1 clove garlic, finely chopped
6 slices bacon, cut into 1-inch pieces
³/₄ cup fat-free cholesterol-free egg product
1 tablespoon olive or vegetable oil
¹/₂ cup freshly grated Parmesan cheese
¹/₂ cup freshly grated Romano cheese
2 tablespoons chopped fresh parsley
¹/₄ teaspoon pepper
Additional freshly grated Parmesan cheese, if desired
Freshly ground pepper, if desired

1 In 4-quart Dutch oven, cook spaghetti as directed on package.

2 Meanwhile, in 10-inch skillet, cook garlic and bacon over medium heat, stirring occasionally, until bacon is crisp; drain.

3 In small bowl, mix egg product, oil, ½ cup Parmesan cheese, the Romano cheese, parsley and ¼ teaspoon pepper.

4 Drain spaghetti; return to Dutch oven. Add bacon mixture and egg product mixture. Cook over low heat, tossing mixture constantly, until egg product coats spaghetti; remove from heat. Serve with additional Parmesan cheese and freshly ground pepper.

1 Serving: Calories 440 (Calories from Fat 110); Total Fat 12g (Saturated Fat 5g); Cholesterol 20mg; Sodium 420mg; Total Carbohydrate 61g (Dietary Fiber 3g); Protein 22g

This recipe uses pasteurized fat-free cholesterol-free egg product instead of traditional raw eggs. This eliminates the risk of contracting salmonella from eating raw or undercooked eggs.

Fettuccine Alfredo

Prep Time: 25 min ▪ Start to Finish: 25 min ▪ 4 servings

Fettuccine
8 oz uncooked fettuccine

Alfredo Sauce
$1/2$ cup butter or margarine
$1/2$ cup heavy whipping cream
$3/4$ cup grated Parmesan cheese
$1/2$ teaspoon salt
Dash of pepper

Garnish
Chopped fresh parsley

1 Cook fettuccine as directed on package.

2 Meanwhile, in 10-inch skillet, heat butter and whipping cream over medium heat, stirring frequently, until butter is melted and mixture starts to bubble; reduce heat to low. Simmer 6 minutes, stirring frequently, until slightly thickened; remove from heat. Stir in cheese, salt and pepper.

3 Drain fettuccine; return to saucepan. Pour sauce over fettuccine; toss until fettuccine is well coated. Sprinkle with parsley.

1 Serving: Calories 550 (Calories from Fat 350); Total Fat 39g (Saturated Fat 25g); Cholesterol 160mg; Sodium 810mg; Total Carbohydrate 38g (Dietary Fiber 2g); Protein 15g

Lighter Fettuccine Alfredo: For 17 grams of fat and 370 calories per serving, decrease butter to $1/4$ cup and Parmesan cheese to $1/2$ cup; substitute evaporated milk for the whipping cream.

Mediterranean Chicken with Rosemary Orzo

Prep Time: 30 min ▪ Start to Finish: 30 min ▪ 4 servings

1 lb chicken breast tenders (not breaded)*
1 can (14 oz) chicken broth
1¹/₃ cups uncooked orzo or rosamarina pasta (about 8 oz)
2 cloves garlic, finely chopped
2 medium zucchini, cut lengthwise into fourths, then cut crosswise
    into slices (1¹/₂ cups)
3 plum (Roma) tomatoes, cut into fourths, sliced (1¹/₂ cups)
1 medium bell pepper, chopped (1 cup)
¹/₂ cup water
1 tablespoon chopped fresh or 1 teaspoon dried rosemary leaves
¹/₂ teaspoon salt

1 Spray 10-inch skillet with cooking spray; heat over medium-high heat. Cook chicken in skillet about 5 minutes, turning occasionally, until brown.

2 Stir in broth, pasta and garlic. Heat to boiling; reduce heat. Cover and simmer about 8 minutes or until most of the liquid is absorbed.

3 Stir in remaining ingredients. Heat to boiling; reduce heat. Simmer uncovered about 5 minutes, stirring once, until bell pepper is crisp-tender and pasta is tender.

*1 lb boneless skinless chicken breasts, cut lengthwise into 1-inch strips, can be substituted for the chicken breast tenders.

1 Serving: Calories 335 (Calories from Fat 45); Total Fat 5g (Saturated Fat 1g); Cholesterol 70mg; Sodium 810mg; Total Carbohydrate 41g (Dietary Fiber 4g); Protein 35g

Chicken Tetrazzini

Prep Time: 20 min ▪ Start to Finish: 50 min ▪ 6 servings

1 package (7 oz) spaghetti, broken into thirds
¼ cup butter or margarine
¼ cup all-purpose flour
½ teaspoon salt
¼ teaspoon pepper
1 cup chicken broth
1 cup heavy whipping cream
2 tablespoons dry sherry or water
2 cups cubed cooked chicken or turkey
1 jar (4.5 oz) sliced mushrooms, drained
½ cup grated Parmesan cheese

1 Heat oven to 350°F. Cook and drain spaghetti as directed on package.

2 Meanwhile, in 2-quart saucepan, melt butter over low heat. Stir in flour, salt and pepper. Cook, stirring constantly, until mixture is smooth and bubbly; remove from heat. Stir in broth and whipping cream. Heat to boiling, stirring constantly. Boil and stir 1 minute.

3 Stir spaghetti, sherry, chicken and mushrooms into sauce. Pour spaghetti mixture into ungreased 2-quart casserole. Sprinkle with cheese.

4 Bake uncovered about 30 minutes or until bubbly in center.

1 Serving: Calories 470 (Calories from Fat 245); Total Fat 27g (Saturated Fat 15g); Cholesterol 110mg; Sodium 610mg; Total Carbohydrate 33g (Dietary Fiber 2g); Protein 24g

Lighter Chicken Tetrazzini: For 10 grams of fat and 320 calories per serving, decrease butter to 2 tablespoons and Parmesan cheese to ¼ cup; substitute fat-free (skim) milk for the whipping cream.

Chicken and Garlic Ravioli with Peppers and Sun-Dried Tomatoes

Prep Time: 30 min ▪ Start to Finish: 30 min ▪ 6 servings

2 packages (9 oz each) refrigerated chicken and roasted garlic-filled ravioli
1/2 cup julienne sun-dried tomatoes in oil and herbs (from 8-oz jar), drained, 2 tablespoons oil reserved
1 bag (1 lb) frozen bell pepper and onion stir-fry, thawed, drained
2 cups shredded provolone cheese (8 oz)

1 Cook and drain ravioli as directed on package.

2 In 12-inch skillet, heat reserved oil over medium heat. Cook bell pepper mixture in oil 2 minutes, stirring occasionally. Stir in tomatoes and ravioli. Cook, stirring occasionally, until hot.

3 Sprinkle with cheese; remove from heat. Cover; let stand 1 to 2 minutes or until cheese is melted.

1 Serving: Calories 390 (Calories from Fat 170); Total Fat 19g (Saturated Fat 8g); Cholesterol 35mg; Sodium 540mg; Total Carbohydrate 35g (Dietary Fiber 3g); Protein 19g

Our best friends are always there for us, as it is with shredded mozzarella cheese—it's a great "pinch hitter" if you don't have provolone.

Spaghetti with White Clam Sauce

Prep Time: 10 min ▪ Start to Finish: 25 min ▪ 4 servings

1 package (7 oz) spaghetti

¼ cup butter or margarine

2 cloves garlic, finely chopped

2 tablespoons chopped fresh parsley

2 cans (6.5 oz each) minced clams, undrained

Additional chopped fresh parsley

½ cup grated Parmesan cheese

1 Cook and drain spaghetti as directed on package.

2 Meanwhile, in 1½-quart saucepan, melt butter over medium heat. Cook garlic in butter about 3 minutes, stirring occasionally, until light golden. Stir in 2 tablespoons parsley and the clams. Heat to boiling; reduce heat. Simmer uncovered 3 to 5 minutes.

3 Drain spaghetti. In large bowl, pour sauce over spaghetti; toss. Sprinkle with additional parsley and cheese.

1 Serving: Calories 485 (Calories from Fat 160); Total Fat 18g (Saturated Fat 10g); Cholesterol 100mg; Sodium 410mg; Total Carbohydrate 45g (Dietary Fiber 2g); Protein 36g

Bow-Ties with Salmon and Tarragon-Mustard Sauce

Prep Time: 30 min ▮ Start to Finish: 30 min ▮ 6 servings

1 package (16 oz) farfalle pasta
1 tablespoon olive oil
1 medium onion, chopped ($^1/_2$ cup)
1 tablespoon chopped fresh tarragon leaves
1 tablespoon chopped fresh parsley
$^1/_4$ cup dry white wine or chicken broth
1 cup heavy whipping cream or half-and-half
2 teaspoons stone-ground mustard
2 packages (3 to 4 oz each) sliced salmon lox (smoked or
    cured), cut into $^1/_2$-inch-wide strips
$^1/_2$ cup freshly grated or shredded Parmesan cheese

1   Cook and drain pasta as directed on package.

2   Meanwhile, in 10-inch skillet, heat oil over medium heat. Cook onion, tarragon and parsley in oil about 5 minutes, stirring frequently, until onion is tender. Add wine. Cook uncovered about 4 minutes or until wine has evaporated. Stir in whipping cream and mustard. Heat to boiling; reduce heat. Simmer uncovered about 10 minutes or until sauce is thickened.

3   Add pasta, salmon and ¼ cup of the cheese to sauce in skillet; toss gently until pasta is evenly coated. Sprinkle with remaining ¼ cup cheese.

1 Serving: Calories 490 (Calories from Fat 180); Total Fat 20g (Saturated Fat 10g); Cholesterol 60mg; Sodium 200mg; Total Carbohydrate 62g (Dietary Fiber 3g); Protein 18g

Parmesan Orzo and Meatballs

Prep Time: 30 min ▪ Start to Finish: 30 min ▪ 4 servings

1½ cups frozen bell pepper and onion stir-fry (from 1-lb bag)
2 tablespoons Italian dressing
1 can (14 oz) beef broth
1 cup uncooked orzo or rosamarina pasta (6 oz)
16 frozen cooked meatballs (from 16-oz bag)
1 large tomato, chopped (1 cup)
2 tablespoons chopped fresh parsley
¼ cup shredded Parmesan cheese (1 oz)

1 In 12-inch nonstick skillet, cook bell pepper mixture and dressing over medium-high heat 2 minutes, stirring frequently.

2 Stir in broth; heat to boiling. Stir in pasta and meatballs. Heat to boiling; reduce heat to low. Cover; cook 10 minutes, stirring occasionally.

3 Stir in tomato. Cover; cook 3 to 5 minutes or until most of liquid has been absorbed and pasta is tender. Stir in parsley. Sprinkle with cheese.

1 Serving: Calories 360 (Calories from Fat 120); Total Fat 14g (Saturated Fat 4.5g); Cholesterol 65mg; Sodium 700mg; Total Carbohydrate 39g (Dietary Fiber 4g); Protein 21g

Orzo is a rice-shaped pasta that cooks fairly quickly. It's also kid-friendly because it is easier to eat than long spaghetti.

Bow-Tie Pasta with Beef and Tomatoes

Prep Time: 20 min ▪ Start to Finish: 20 min ▪ 4 servings

2 cups uncooked bow-tie (farfalle) pasta (4 oz)
1 tablespoon olive or vegetable oil
1 cup frozen bell pepper and onion stir-fry (from 1-lb bag)
1 lb beef strips for stir-fry or thinly sliced flank steak
1 can (14.5 oz) Italian-style stewed tomatoes, undrained
1 teaspoon garlic salt
$1/4$ teaspoon pepper
Fresh basil leaves, if desired
Freshly shredded Parmesan cheese, if desired

1 Cook and drain pasta as directed on package.

2 Meanwhile, in 12-inch skillet, heat oil over medium-high heat. Cook bell pepper mixture in oil 3 minutes, stirring frequently. Stir in beef. Cook 5 to 6 minutes, stirring frequently, until beef is no longer pink.

3 Stir in tomatoes, garlic salt and pepper. Cook 2 to 3 minutes, stirring frequently and breaking up tomatoes slightly with spoon, until mixture is hot. Stir in pasta. Cook 1 to 2 minutes, stirring constantly, until pasta is well coated and hot. Garnish with basil. Serve with cheese.

1 Serving: Calories 350 (Calories from Fat 110); Total Fat 12g (Saturated Fat 3.5g); Cholesterol 50mg; Sodium 520mg; Total Carbohydrate 29g (Dietary Fiber 3g); Protein 31g

This handy one-dish pasta recipe is already fast, but it's even faster (and handier) if you substitute leftover cold pasta you might have in the fridge for the uncooked pasta. No need to warm it up first; just heat it an extra minute or two after stirring into the sauce.

Stove-Top Lasagna

Prep Time: 20 min ▪ Start to Finish: 20 min ▪ 6 servings

1 lb bulk Italian sausage
1 medium green bell pepper, sliced
1 package (8 oz) sliced mushrooms (3 cups)
1 medium onion, chopped (½ cup)
3 cups uncooked mini lasagna (mafalda) noodles (6 oz)
2½ cups water
½ teaspoon Italian seasoning
1 jar (26 oz) chunky tomato pasta sauce (any variety)
1 cup shredded Italian cheese blend or mozzarella cheese (4 oz)

1 In 12-inch skillet or 4-quart Dutch oven, cook sausage, bell pepper, mushrooms and onion over medium-high heat, stirring occasionally, until sausage is no longer pink; drain.

2 Stir in remaining ingredients except cheese. Heat to boiling, stirring occasionally; reduce heat. Simmer uncovered about 10 minutes or until pasta is tender. Sprinkle with cheese.

1 Serving: Calories 500 (Calories from Fat 210); Total Fat 24g (Saturated Fat 9g); Cholesterol 60mg; Sodium 1260mg; Total Carbohydrate 50g (Dietary Fiber 5g); Protein 22g

Crumble, cook and drain sausage ahead to save time. Cooked and drained ground beef is a quick substitution for the sausage in this easy lasagna.

Classic Meat Sauce

Prep Time: 1 hr 15 min ▪ Start to Finish: 1 hr 15 min ▪ 12 servings

2 tablespoons olive oil

2 tablespoons butter or margarine

2 medium carrots, finely chopped (1 cup)

1 medium onion, chopped ($^1/_2$ cup)

$^1/_2$ lb bulk Italian sausage

$^1/_2$ lb lean ground beef

3 cans (28 oz each) Italian-style plum (Roma) tomatoes, drained, chopped

$^1/_2$ cup dry red wine or beef broth

1 teaspoon salt

1 teaspoon dried oregano leaves

$^1/_2$ teaspoon pepper

1 In 4-quart Dutch oven, heat oil and butter over medium-high heat until butter is melted. Cook carrots and onion in oil mixture about 8 minutes, stirring occasionally, until carrots and onion are tender.

2 Stir in sausage and beef. Reduce heat to medium. Cook, stirring occasionally, until sausage is no longer pink and beef is brown; drain.

3 Stir in remaining ingredients. Heat to boiling; reduce heat to low. Cover and simmer 45 minutes, stirring occasionally.

4 Use sauce immediately, or tightly cover and refrigerate up to 48 hours or freeze up to 2 months.

1 Serving ($^1/_2$ cup): Calories 170 (Calories from Fat 100); Total Fat 11g (Saturated Fat 4g); Cholesterol 25mg; Sodium 640mg; Total Carbohydrate 11g (Dietary Fiber 2g); Protein 8g

Classic Tomato Sauce

Prep Time: 1 hr ▪ Start to Finish: 1 hr ▪ 5 servings

1 tablespoon olive oil
4 cloves garlic, finely chopped
1 small onion, chopped ($^1/_4$ cup)
2 cans (28 oz each) Italian-style pear-shaped (plum) tomatoes, drained
2 tablespoons chopped fresh or 2 teaspoons dried basil leaves
2 tablespoons chopped fresh or 2 teaspoons dried oregano leaves
$^1/_2$ teaspoon salt
$^1/_2$ teaspoon pepper

1 In 3-quart saucepan, heat oil over medium-high heat. Cook garlic and onion in oil about 5 minutes, stirring frequently, until onion is tender.

2 Place tomatoes in food processor or blender. Cover and process until smooth. Stir tomatoes and remaining ingredients into onion mixture. Heat to boiling; reduce heat. Simmer uncovered 45 minutes, stirring occasionally.

3 Use sauce immediately, or tightly cover and refrigerate up to 48 hours or freeze up to 2 months.

1 Serving ($^1/_2$ cup): Calories 50 (Calories from Fat 20); Total Fat 2g (Saturated Fat 0g); Cholesterol 0mg; Sodium 380mg; Total Carbohydrate 8g (Dietary Fiber 2g); Protein 2g

Tomato-Cream Sauce

Prep Time: 35 min ▪ Start to Finish: 35 min ▪ 4 servings

1 tablespoon olive oil
1 clove garlic, finely chopped
1 medium onion, chopped (1/2 cup)
1 tablespoon chopped fresh parsley or 1 teaspoon parsley flakes
1 tablespoon chopped fresh or 1 teaspoon dried basil leaves
1 can (28 oz) Italian-style plum (Roma) tomatoes, drained and chopped
1/2 cup heavy whipping cream
1/2 teaspoon ground nutmeg
1/4 teaspoon salt
1/8 teaspoon pepper

1 In 12-inch skillet, heat oil over medium-high heat. Cook garlic, onion, parsley, basil and tomatoes in oil 10 minutes, stirring occasionally.

2 Stir in remaining ingredients. Cook about 20 minutes, stirring occasionally, until sauce is thickened.

3 Use sauce immediately, or tightly cover and refrigerate up to 24 hours. Freezing is not recommended because sauce will separate when reheated.

1 Serving (1/2 cup): Calories 165 (Calories from Fat 115); Total Fat 13g (Saturated Fat 6g); Cholesterol 35mg; Sodium 450mg; Total Carbohydrate 12g (Dietary Fiber 3g); Protein 3g

Basil Pesto

Prep Time: 10 min   Start to Finish: 10 min   10 servings

2 cups firmly packed fresh basil leaves
³/₄ cup grated Parmesan cheese
¹/₄ cup pine nuts
¹/₂ cup olive or vegetable oil
3 cloves garlic

1 In blender or food processor, place all ingredients. Cover and blend on medium speed about 3 minutes, stopping occasionally to scrape sides, until smooth.

2 Use pesto immediately, or cover tightly and refrigerate up to 5 days or freeze up to 1 month (color of pesto will darken as it stands).

1 Serving (2 tablespoons): Calories 150 (Calories From Fat 135); Total Fat 15g (Saturated Fat 3g); Cholesterol 5mg; Sodium 140mg; Total Carbohydrate 2g (Dietary Fiber 1g); Protein 3g

Cilantro Pesto: Substitute 1½ cups firmly packed fresh cilantro and ½ cup firmly packed fresh parsley for the basil.

Sun-Dried Tomato Pesto: Use food processor. Omit basil. Decrease oil to ⅓ cup; add ½ cup oil-packed sun-dried tomatoes (undrained).

Winter Spinach Pesto: Substitute 2 cups firmly packed fresh spinach and ½ cup firmly packed fresh basil leaves or ¼ cup dried basil leaves for the fresh basil.

Classic Risotto

Prep Time: 35 min ■ Start to Finish: 35 min ■ 4 servings

1 tablespoon butter or margarine
2 tablespoons olive or vegetable oil
1 small onion, thinly sliced
1 tablespoon chopped fresh parsley
1 cup uncooked Arborio or regular long-grain rice
$^{1}/_{2}$ cup dry white wine or chicken broth
3 cups chicken broth, warmed
$^{1}/_{2}$ cup freshly grated or shredded Parmesan cheese
$^{1}/_{4}$ teaspoon coarsely ground pepper

1 In nonstick 10-inch skillet or 3-quart saucepan, heat butter and oil over medium-high heat until butter is melted. Cook onion and parsley in oil mixture about 5 minutes, stirring frequently, until onion is tender.

2 Stir in rice. Cook, stirring occasionally, until edges of kernels are translucent. Stir in wine. Cook about 3 minutes, stirring constantly, until wine is absorbed.

3 Reduce heat to medium. Stir in 1 cup of the broth. Cook uncovered about 5 minutes, stirring frequently, until broth is absorbed. Repeat, adding another 1 cup of broth. Stir in remaining 1 cup broth. Cook about 8 minutes, stirring frequently, until rice is just tender and mixture is creamy.

4 Stir in cheese and pepper.

1 Serving: Calories 355 (Calories from Fat 135); Total Fat 15g (Saturated Fat 5g); Cholesterol 15mg; Sodium 1020mg; Total Carbohydrate 43g (Fiber 1g); Protein 13g

Classic Risotto with Peas: Just before serving, stir in 1 box (9 oz) frozen green peas, cooked and drained.

Risotto with Shrimp

Prep Time: 1 hr ▪ Start to Finish: 1 hr ▪ 4 servings

2 tablespoons butter or margarine

1 medium onion, thinly sliced

1 lb uncooked medium shrimp, peeled (tails shells removed), deveined

1½ cups uncooked Arborio or regular long-grain rice

½ cup dry white wine or chicken broth

3 cups chicken broth, warmed

¼ teaspoon coarsely ground pepper

¼ cup freshly grated or shredded Parmesan cheese

1 In nonstick 12-inch skillet or Dutch oven, melt butter over medium-high heat. Cook onion in butter about 8 minutes, stirring frequently, until tender.

2 Reduce heat to medium. Stir in shrimp. Cook uncovered about 8 minutes, turning once, until shrimp are pink. Remove shrimp from skillet; keep warm.

3 Add rice to skillet. Cook about 5 minutes, stirring occasionally, until edges of kernels are translucent. Stir in wine. Cook about 3 minutes, stirring constantly, until wine is absorbed.

4 Stir in ½ cup of the broth. Cook uncovered about 5 minutes, stirring occasionally, until broth is absorbed. Stir in remaining broth, ½ cup at a time, cooking about 3 minutes after each addition and stirring occasionally, until broth is absorbed, rice is just tender and mixture is creamy.

5 Stir in shrimp and pepper. Sprinkle with cheese.

1 Serving: Calories 220 (Calories from Fat 45); Total Fat 5g (Saturated Fat 3g); Cholesterol 65mg; Sodium 530mg; Total Carbohydrate 32g (Dietary Fiber 1g); Protein 12g

Three-Mushroom Risotto

Prep Time: 35 min ▪ Start to Finish: 1 hr 35 min ▪ 3 servings

1 package (about 1.25 oz) dried porcini mushrooms (about 1 cup)
$1/4$ cup olive oil
2 tablespoons chopped fresh parsley
4 cloves garlic, finely chopped
2 medium green onions, sliced (2 tablespoons)
1 cup uncooked Arborio rice or regular long-grain rice
1 package (about 3.5 oz) fresh shiitake mushrooms, thinly sliced
1 package (about 5.5 oz) fresh crimini mushrooms, thinly sliced
$3^1/2$ cups chicken broth, warmed
$1/2$ cup freshly grated or shredded Parmesan cheese
1 tablespoon balsamic vinegar

1 In small bowl, cover porcini mushrooms with warm water. Let stand at room temperature about 1 hour or until tender; drain.

2 In 10-inch nonstick skillet, heat oil over medium-high heat. Cook parsley, garlic and onions in oil about 5 minutes, stirring frequently, until onions are tender.

3 Stir in rice. Cook, stirring, until edges of kernels are translucent. Stir in porcini, shiitake and crimini mushrooms. Cook uncovered about 3 minutes, stirring frequently, until mushrooms are tender.

4 Reduce heat to medium. Add 1 cup of the broth. Cook uncovered about 5 minutes, stirring frequently, until broth is absorbed. Stir in remaining broth, ½ cup at a time, cooking about 3 minutes after each addition and stirring occasionally, until broth is absorbed, rice is just tender and mixture is moist.

5 Stir in cheese and vinegar.

1 Serving: Calories 275 (Calories from Fat 115); Total Fat 13g (Saturated Fat 3g); Cholesterol 5mg; Sodium 770mg; Total Carbohydrate 31g (Dietary Fiber 1g); Protein 10g

Beef Stew, Bologna Style

Beef Roast with Parmesan and Cream

Grilled Steak, Florentine Style

Grilled Meatball Kabobs

Veal Saltimbocca

Pork Roast with Rosemary

Peppered Pork Chops

Pork Tenderloin with Prosciutto

New-Style Pork Chops

Roasted Chicken with Lemon and Herbs

Chicken in Olive-Wine Sauce

Chicken Baked with Artichokes and Potatoes

Chicken with Spicy Red and Yellow Pepper Sauce

Chicken Piccata

Chicken Milanese

Chicken Cacciatore

Chicken Marsala

Bass with Parmesan

Shrimp Scampi

Grilled Shrimp Kabobs with Fresh Herbs

Spicy Breaded Shrimp

4

main courses

Beef Stew, Bologna Style

Prep Time: 1 hr 25 min ■ Start to Finish: 1 hr 25 min ■ 6 servings

1½ lb beef boneless sirloin steak, about 1 inch thick

1 tablespoon olive oil

4 oz sliced pancetta or lean bacon, cut into ½-inch pieces

1 medium onion, chopped (½ cup)

1 medium green bell pepper, chopped (1 cup)

2 cloves garlic, finely chopped

1 tablespoon chopped fresh parsley

1 cup sweet red wine or beef broth

1 tablespoon balsamic vinegar

¼ teaspoon salt

¼ teaspoon pepper

2 medium potatoes, cut into 1-inch pieces

1 medium carrot, thinly sliced (½ cup)

2 fresh or dried bay leaves

1 Remove fat from beef. Cut beef into 1-inch cubes.

2 In nonstick 4-quart Dutch oven, heat oil over medium heat. Cook pancetta, onion, bell pepper, garlic and parsley in oil about 10 minutes, stirring occasionally, until pancetta is brown.

3 Stir in beef and remaining ingredients. Heat to boiling; reduce heat. Cover and simmer about 1 hour, stirring occasionally, until beef is tender. Remove bay leaves.

1 Serving: Calories 220 (Calories from Fat 65); Total Fat 7g (Saturated Fat 2g); Cholesterol 60mg; Sodium 390mg; Total Carbohydrate 15g (Dietary Fiber 2g); Protein 25g

Beef Roast with Parmesan and Cream

Prep Time: 2 hr 35 min ■ Start to Finish: 2 hr 35 min ■ 10 servings

3-lb beef boneless rump roast
2 oz Parmesan cheese, cut into 2 × ¹/₄ × ¹/₄-inch strips
2 tablespoons butter or margarine
2 tablespoons olive oil
¹/₂ teaspoon salt
¹/₂ teaspoon pepper
¹/₂ cup dry red wine or beef broth
1 cup heavy whipping cream
¹/₂ cup freshly grated Parmesan cheese

1 Make small, deep cuts in all sides of beef with sharp knife. Insert 1 cheese strip completely into each cut.

2 In 4-quart Dutch oven, heat butter and oil over medium-high heat until butter is melted. Cook beef in butter mixture, turning occasionally, until brown on all sides. Sprinkle beef with salt and pepper. Add wine. Cook uncovered about 5 minutes or until liquid has evaporated.

3 Pour whipping cream over beef; reduce heat. Cover and simmer about 2 hours or until beef is tender.

4 Place beef on warm platter; cover loosely with tent of foil to keep warm. Skim fat from juices in Dutch oven. Stir grated cheese into juices. Heat to boiling over medium heat, stirring constantly and scraping particles from bottom of pan. Cut beef into thin slices. Serve with cream sauce.

1 Serving: Calories 295 (Calories from Fat 170); Total Fat 19g (Saturated Fat 10g); Cholesterol 105mg; Sodium 420mg; Total Carbohydrate 1g (Dietary Fiber 0g); Protein 30g

Grilled Steak, Florentine Style

Prep Time: 20 min ▪ Start to Finish: 20 min ▪ 4 servings

¼ cup chopped fresh parsley
¼ cup olive oil
4 cloves garlic, cut into pieces
4 beef T-bone steaks, about 1 inch thick (8 oz each)
1 teaspoon salt
½ teaspoon freshly ground pepper

1 Brush grill rack with olive or vegetable oil. Heat gas or charcoal grill.

2 Place parsley, oil and garlic in food processor or blender. Cover and process until smooth.

3 Cut outer edge of fat on beef steaks diagonally at 1-inch intervals to prevent curling (do not cut into beef).

4 Cover and grill beef 3 to 4 inches from medium heat 5 minutes for medium-rare or 7 minutes for medium, brushing frequently with oil mixture. Turn; brush generously with oil mixture. Grill 5 to 7 minutes longer until desired doneness. Sprinkle with salt and pepper. Discard any remaining oil mixture.

1 Serving: Calories 330 (Calories from Fat 205); Total Fat 23g (Saturated Fat 5g); Cholesterol 80mg; Sodium 660mg; Total Carbohydrate 1g (Dietary Fiber 0g); Protein 30g

Grilled Meatball Kabobs

Prep Time: 35 min ■ Start to Finish: 35 min ■ 4 servings

1 lb ground beef, pork and veal mixture (meat loaf mixture)
1 tablespoon chopped fresh parsley
1 tablespoon chopped fresh or 1 teaspoon dried basil leaves
1 teaspoon salt
1/4 teaspoon pepper
1 small onion, finely chopped (1/4 cup)
2 cloves garlic, finely chopped
1 egg
2 large green bell peppers, cut into 1-inch squares

1 Brush grill rack with olive or vegetable oil. Heat gas or charcoal grill.

2 In large bowl, mix all ingredients except bell peppers. Shape mixture into 1-inch balls. Thread meatballs and bell pepper squares alternately on each of four 12-inch metal skewers, leaving space between each piece.

3 Cover and grill kabobs about 4 inches from medium heat about 10 minutes, turning frequently, until meatballs are no longer pink in center.

1 Serving: Calories 240 (Calories from Fat 125); Total Fat 14g (Saturated Fat 5g); Cholesterol 125mg; Sodium 660mg; Total Carbohydrate 7g (Dietary Fiber 2g); Protein 23g

Broiled Meatball Kabobs: Set oven control to broil. Brush broiler pan rack with olive or vegetable oil. Broil with tops about 3 inches from heat 5 minutes; turn kabobs. Broil 4 to 5 minutes longer or until meatballs are no longer pink in center.

Veal Saltimbocca

Prep Time: 25 min ■ Start to Finish: 25 min ■ 4 servings

8 veal top round or round steaks, $1/4$ inch thick (about $1^1/_2$ lb)
$1/_2$ cup all-purpose flour
8 thin slices prosciutto or fully cooked ham
8 thin slices (1 oz each) mozzarella cheese
8 fresh sage leaves
$1/_4$ cup butter or margarine
$1/_2$ cup dry white wine or chicken broth
$1/_2$ teaspoon salt
$1/_4$ teaspoon pepper

1 Lightly pound each veal steak with meat mallet to tenderize and to flatten slightly. Coat veal with flour; shake off excess. Layer 1 slice each of prosciutto and cheese and 1 sage leaf on each veal slice. Roll up veal; tie with butcher string or secure with toothpicks.

2 In 10-inch skillet, melt butter over medium heat. Cook veal rolls in butter about 5 minutes, turning occasionally, until brown. Add wine; sprinkle rolls with salt and pepper. Cover and cook over medium-high heat about 5 minutes or until veal is of desired doneness.

1 Serving: Calories 550 (Calories from Fat 240); Total Fat 30g (Saturated Fat 17g); Cholesterol 190mg; Sodium 1190mg; Total Carbohydrate 15g (Dietary Fiber 1g); Protein 50g

Pork Roast with Rosemary

Prep Time: 15 min ▪ Start to Finish: 1 hr 50 min ▪ 8 servings

2 tablespoons chopped fresh or
2 teaspoons dried rosemary leaves, crumbled
4 cloves garlic, finely chopped
3- to 3½-lb pork loin center roast (bone-in)
1 teaspoon salt
½ teaspoon pepper
1 tablespoon butter or margarine
1 small onion, chopped (¼ cup)
2 tablespoons olive oil

1 Heat oven to 325°F. In small bowl, mix rosemary and garlic. Make 8 to 10 deep cuts about 2 inches apart in all sides of pork with sharp knife. Place small amount of rosemary mixture in each cut. Sprinkle pork with salt and pepper.

2 In shallow roasting pan, melt butter in oven; sprinkle with onion. Place pork in pan; drizzle with oil. Insert meat thermometer so tip is in center of thickest part of pork and does not rest in fat. Roast uncovered about 1 hour 15 minutes or until thermometer reads 155°F. Remove from oven; cover with tent of foil and let stand 15 to 20 minutes or until temperature rises to 160°F (medium).

1 Serving: Calories 225 (Calories from Fat 115); Total Fat 13g (Saturated Fat 4g); Cholesterol 75mg; Sodium 350mg; Total Carbohydrate 1g (Dietary Fiber 0g); Protein 26g

Peppered Pork Chops

Prep Time: 40 min ▪ Start to Finish: 40 min ▪ 6 servings

1 tablespoon whole black peppercorns, coarsely crushed
6 pork loin chops, ³/₄ inch thick (about 2 lb)
2 tablespoons butter or margarine
2 tablespoons olive oil
4 cloves garlic, cut in half
1 cup sliced mushrooms (3 oz)
¹/₂ teaspoon salt
¹/₂ cup dry Marsala wine, dry red wine or beef broth

1 Sprinkle half of the crushed peppercorns over one side of pork chops; gently press into pork. Turn pork; repeat with remaining peppercorns.

2 In 12-inch skillet, heat butter and oil over medium-high heat until butter is melted. Cook garlic in butter mixture, stirring frequently, until golden. Cook pork in butter mixture about 5 minutes or until brown; turn pork.

3 Add mushrooms, salt and wine; reduce heat. Cover and simmer about 15 minutes or until pork is no longer pink and meat thermometer inserted in center reads 160°F.

1 Serving: Calories 260 (Calories from Fat 155); Total Fat 17g (Saturated Fat 6g); Cholesterol 75mg; Sodium 280mg; Total Carbohydrate 2g (Dietary Fiber 0g); Protein 24g

Pork Tenderloin with Prosciutto

Prep Time: 45 min ■ Start to Finish: 45 min ■ 6 servings

1½ lb pork tenderloin
2 tablespoons olive oil
¼ cup chopped prosciutto or fully cooked ham (about 2 oz)
2 tablespoons chopped fresh sage leaves
2 tablespoons chopped fresh parsley
2 tablespoons chopped sun-dried tomatoes in oil
1 small onion, chopped (¼ cup)
½ cup dry white wine or chicken broth
½ cup heavy whipping cream or half-and-half
½ teaspoon pepper
¼ teaspoon salt

1 Cut pork diagonally across grain into ½-inch slices. In 12-inch skillet, heat oil over medium-high heat. Cook prosciutto, sage, parsley, tomatoes and onion in oil about 5 minutes, stirring frequently, until onion is tender.

2 Add pork to skillet. Cook about 10 minutes, turning pork occasionally, until pork is light brown. Stir in remaining ingredients. Heat to boiling; reduce heat. Simmer uncovered about 20 minutes, stirring occasionally, until pork is no longer pink in center and sauce is thickened.

1 Serving: Calories 255 (Calories from Fat 145); Total Fat 16g (Saturated Fat 6g); Cholesterol 90mg; Sodium 290mg; Total Carbohydrate 3g (Dietary Fiber 1g); Protein 26g

Italian prosciutto, slowly cured and aged, is usually sweet tasting and is an ideal accompaniment to appetizers and other meat dishes. In this recipe, it marries well with the subtle yet zealous flavor of sun-dried tomatoes. Italian cooks enjoy simple, natural flavors such as these, and you can too!

New-Style Pork Chops

Prep Time: 55 min ■ Start to Finish: 8 hr 55 min ■ 6 servings

6 pork loin or rib chops, about 1 inch thick (about 2 lb)
1 cup dry Marsala wine, dry red wine or beef broth
1 tablespoon balsamic vinegar
1 tablespoon fresh lemon juice
1 teaspoon honey
2 tablespoons olive oil
1 tablespoon chopped fresh thyme leaves
1 tablespoon chopped fresh parsley
$1/2$ teaspoon salt
$1/2$ teaspoon pepper
1 cup Kalamata olives, pitted
1 medium red onion, chopped ($1/2$ cup)
2 cloves garlic, finely chopped

1 Place pork in shallow glass or plastic dish. In small bowl, mix wine, vinegar, lemon juice and honey; pour over pork. Turn pork to coat both sides. Cover and refrigerate at least 8 hours but no longer than 24 hours, turning occasionally.

2 In 12-inch skillet, heat oil over medium-high heat. Cook remaining ingredients in oil about 5 minutes, stirring frequently, until onion is tender.

3 Remove pork from marinade; reserve marinade. Add pork to skillet. Cook about 10 minutes, turning pork once, until pork is brown. Add reserved marinade. Heat to boiling; reduce heat. Cover and simmer about 20 minutes or until pork is no longer pink and meat thermometer inserted in center reads 160°F. Serve pork with pan sauce.

1 Serving: Calories 230 (Calories from Fat 115); Total Fat 13g (Saturated Fat 3g); Cholesterol 65mg; Sodium 430mg; Total Carbohydrate 6g (Dietary Fiber 1g); Protein 23g

Roasted Chicken with Lemon and Herbs

Prep Time: 15 min ▪ Start to Finish: 2 hr ▪ 6 servings

4 cloves garlic, finely chopped
1 tablespoon chopped fresh flat-leaf or curly parsley
1 tablespoon chopped fresh sage leaves
1 tablespoon chopped fresh chives
3- to 3 1/2-lb whole broiler-fryer chicken
1 lemon, cut in half
2 tablespoons olive oil
1/2 teaspoon salt
1/4 teaspoon pepper

1 Heat oven to 375°F. In small bowl, mix garlic, parsley, sage and chives.

2 Fold wings of chicken across back with tips touching. Make several 1-inch-deep cuts in chicken. Insert about 1/2 teaspoon herb mixture in each cut until all herb mixture is used. Rub lemon halves over skin of the chicken. Squeeze remaining juice from lemon halves; set aside.

3 Tie or skewer drumsticks to tail. Place chicken, breast side up, on rack in shallow roasting pan. Drizzle oil over chicken; sprinkle with salt and pepper. Insert ovenproof meat thermometer so tip is in thickest part of inside thigh and does not touch bone.

4 Roast uncovered 1 hour to 1 hour 30 minutes, brushing occasionally with remaining lemon juice, until thermometer reads 180°F and legs move easily when lifted or twisted. Remove from oven; let stand about 15 minutes for easiest carving.

1 Serving: Calories 255 (Calories from Fat 145); Total Fat 16g (Saturated Fat 4g); Cholesterol 85mg; Sodium 280mg; Total Carbohydrate 1g (Dietary Fiber 0g); Protein 27g

Chicken in Olive-Wine Sauce

Prep Time: 35 min ■ Start to Finish: 35 min ■ 4 servings

2 slices bacon, cut into 1-inch pieces
1 medium onion, chopped ($^1/_2$ cup)
2 cloves garlic, finely chopped
1 tablespoon chopped fresh or 1 teaspoon dried rosemary leaves, crumbled
4 boneless skinless chicken breasts (about 1$^1/_4$ lb)
$^1/_2$ cup pimiento-stuffed olives
$^1/_2$ cup dry red wine or chicken broth
1 cup seasoned croutons
1 tablespoon chopped fresh parsley

1 In 10-inch skillet, cook bacon, onion, garlic and rosemary over medium-high heat about 8 minutes, stirring occasionally, until bacon is crisp. Remove bacon with slotted spoon; set aside.

2 Add chicken to skillet. Cook about 5 minutes, turning frequently, until chicken is brown. Add olives, wine and bacon. Cover and cook about 12 minutes or until juice of chicken is clear when center of thickest part is cut (170°F).

3 Place chicken on serving platter. Sprinkle with croutons and parsley.

1 Serving: Calories 270 (Calories from Fat 80); Total Fat 9g (Saturated Fat 2g); Cholesterol 90mg; Sodium 620mg; Total Carbohydrate 9g (Dietary Fiber 1g); Protein 34g

Chicken Baked with Artichokes and Potatoes

Prep Time: 15 min ■ Start to Finish: 1 hr 15 min ■ 6 servings

2 tablespoons olive oil

1/2 lb chicken livers, chopped

1 medium onion, chopped (1/2 cup)

2 cloves garlic, finely chopped

2 tablespoons chopped fresh or 1 teaspoon dried sage leaves, crumbled

1 tablespoon chopped fresh parsley

1 tablespoon capers

1 can (14 oz) artichoke hearts, drained, cut into fourths

3- to 3 1/2-lb cut-up broiler-fryer chicken

1 1/2 lb new potatoes (10 to 12), cut into 1-inch pieces

1/2 cup dry white wine or chicken broth

2 tablespoons fresh lemon juice

1 teaspoon salt

1 teaspoon freshly ground pepper

1 Heat oven to 425°F. In 10-inch skillet, heat oil over medium-high heat. Cook livers, onion, garlic, sage, parsley and capers in oil about 8 minutes, stirring frequently, until livers are no longer red. Spread liver mixture in ungreased 13 × 9-inch pan.

2 Spread artichokes over liver mixture. Place chicken, skin sides down, and potatoes on artichokes. Mix wine and lemon juice; pour over chicken and potatoes. Sprinkle with salt and pepper.

3 Bake uncovered 30 minutes. Turn chicken and potatoes. Bake about 30 minutes longer or until chicken is brown on outside and juice of chicken is clear when thickest piece is cut to bone (170°F for breasts; 180°F for thighs and drumsticks).

1 Serving: Calories 400 (Calories from Fat 160); Total Fat 18g (Saturated Fat 5g); Cholesterol 230mg; Sodium 720mg; Total Carbohydrate 27g (Dietary Fiber 6g); Protein 36g

Chicken with Spicy Red and Yellow Pepper Sauce

Prep Time: 15 min ■ Start to Finish: 1 hr 15 min ■ 6 servings

3- to 3½-lb cut-up broiler-fryer
   chicken
½ cup all-purpose flour
¼ cup chopped fresh parsley
1 tablespoon chopped anchovy
   fillets in oil
1 teaspoon crushed red pepper
2 cloves garlic, finely chopped
2 tablespoons olive oil

1 large red bell pepper, cut into
   1-inch pieces
1 large yellow bell pepper, cut into
   1-inch pieces
1 tablespoon chopped fresh or
   1 teaspoon dried basil leaves
½ cup dry white wine or chicken
   broth
1 teaspoon salt

1 Heat oven to 375°F. Coat chicken with flour; shake off excess flour.

2 In small bowl, mix parsley, anchovies, red pepper and garlic. In 12-inch skillet, heat oil over medium-high heat. Cook parsley mixture in oil 5 minutes, stirring frequently. Add chicken. Cook about 10 minutes, turning once, until chicken is lightly browned on all sides.

3 Place chicken, skin sides down, in ungreased 13 × 9-inch pan. Arrange bell peppers around chicken. Sprinkle basil over chicken and bell peppers.

4 Add wine to skillet. Heat to boiling, stirring constantly to loosen particles on bottom of skillet; pour over chicken and peppers. Sprinkle with salt.

5 Bake uncovered 30 minutes. Turn chicken. Bake about 30 minutes longer or until juice of chicken is clear when thickest piece is cut to bone (170°F for breasts; 180°F for thighs and drumsticks).

1 Serving: Calories 320 (Calories from Fat 155); Total Fat 17g (Saturated Fat 4g); Cholesterol 85mg; Sodium 570mg; Total Carbohydrate 12g (Dietary Fiber 1g); Protein 29g

Chicken Piccata

Prep Time: 30 min ▪ Start to Finish: 30 min ▪ 4 servings

4 boneless skinless chicken breasts (about 1¼ lb)
⅓ cup all-purpose flour
¼ cup butter or margarine
2 cloves garlic, finely chopped
1 cup dry white wine or chicken broth
2 tablespoons fresh lemon juice
¼ teaspoon pepper
1 tablespoon capers

1 Between pieces of plastic wrap or waxed paper, place each chicken breast smooth side down; gently pound with flat side of meat mallet or rolling pin until ¼ inch thick. Coat chicken with flour; shake off excess flour.

2 In 12-inch skillet, melt butter over medium-high heat. Cook chicken and garlic in butter about 6 minutes, turning once, until chicken is brown.

3 Add wine and lemon juice; reduce heat to medium. Sprinkle chicken with pepper. Cook 8 to 10 minutes, turning once, until chicken is no longer pink in center. Sprinkle with capers.

1 Serving: Calories 340 (Calories from Fat 145); Total Fat 16g (Saturated Fat 8g); Cholesterol 115mg; Sodium 220mg; Total Carbohydrate 8g (Dietary Fiber 0g); Protein 32g

Veal in Lemon-Caper Sauce: Substitute 1½ pounds veal for scallopini, (about ¼ inch thick) for the chicken. Decrease wine to ½ cup. Make as directed above—except after adding wine and lemon juice, heat just until hot (do not cook 8 to 10 minutes). Sprinkle with capers.

Chicken Milanese

Prep Time: 35 min ■ Start to Finish: 35 min ■ 6 servings

6 boneless skinless chicken breast (about 1³/₄ lb)
½ teaspoon salt
¼ teaspoon pepper
2 eggs, beaten
1 tablespoon fresh lemon juice
⅓ cup all-purpose flour
1 cup Italian-style dry bread crumbs
½ cup butter or margarine
1 lemon, cut into wedges
Chopped fresh parsley or parsley sprigs, if desired

1 Between pieces of plastic wrap or waxed paper, place each chicken breast smooth side down; gently pound with flat side of meat mallet or rolling pin until ¼ inch thick. Sprinkle with salt and pepper. In small bowl, mix eggs and lemon juice. Coat chicken with flour; shake off excess flour. Dip chicken into egg mixture, then coat with bread crumbs; shake off excess crumbs.

2 In 12-inch skillet, melt butter over medium heat. Cook chicken in butter 10 to 15 minutes, turning once, until chicken is golden brown on outside and no longer pink in center.

3 Place chicken on warm platter; pour any remaining butter from skillet over chicken. Garnish with lemon wedges and parsley.

1 Serving: Calories 390 (Calories from Fat 200); Total Fat 22g (Saturated Fat 11g); Cholesterol 190mg; Sodium 530mg; Total Carbohydrate 16g (Dietary Fiber 1g); Protein 33g

Veal Milanese: Substitute 6 veal cutlets, about ½ inch thick, for the chicken. Make as directed—except do not flatten; cook in butter about 8 minutes, turning once, until veal is of desired doneness.

Chicken Cacciatore

Prep Time: 1 hr 20 min ■ Start to Finish: 1 hr 20 min ■ 6 servings

3- to 3½-lb cut-up whole chicken
½ cup all-purpose flour
¼ cup vegetable oil
1 medium green bell pepper
2 medium onions
1 can (14.5 oz) diced tomatoes, undrained
1 can (8 oz) tomato sauce
1 cup sliced fresh mushrooms (3 oz)
1½ teaspoons chopped fresh or ½ teaspoon dried oregano leaves
1 teaspoon chopped fresh or ¼ teaspoon dried basil leaves
½ teaspoon salt
2 cloves garlic, finely chopped
Grated Parmesan cheese, if desired

1 Coat chicken with flour. In 12-inch skillet, heat oil over medium-high heat. Cook chicken in oil 15 to 20 minutes or until brown on all sides; drain.

2 Cut bell pepper and onions crosswise in half; cut each half into fourths.

3 Stir bell pepper, onions and remaining ingredients except cheese into chicken in skillet. Heat to boiling; reduce heat. Cover and simmer 30 to 40 minutes or until juice of chicken is clear when thickest piece is cut to bone (170°F for breasts; 180°F for thighs and drumsticks). Serve with cheese.

1 Serving: Calories 400 (Calories from Fat 205); Total Fat 23g (Saturated Fat 5g); Cholesterol 85mg; Sodium 620mg; Total Carbohydrate 19g (Dietary Fiber 3g); Pro. 30g

Chicken Marsala

Prep Time: 35 min ■ Start to Finish: 35 min ■ 4 servings

4 boneless skinless chicken breasts (about 1¼ lb)
½ cup all-purpose flour
¼ teaspoon salt
¼ teaspoon pepper
2 tablespoons olive or vegetable oil
2 cloves garlic, finely chopped
1 cup sliced fresh mushrooms (3 oz)
¼ cup chopped fresh parsley or 1 tablespoon parsley flakes
½ cup dry Marsala wine or chicken broth
Hot cooked pasta, if desired

1 Between pieces of plastic wrap or waxed paper, place each chicken breast smooth side down; gently pound with flat side of meat mallet or rolling pin until ¼ inch thick. In shallow dish, mix flour, salt and pepper. Coat chicken with flour mixture; shake off excess flour.

2 In 10-inch skillet, heat oil over medium-high heat. Cook garlic, mushrooms and parsley in oil 5 minutes, stirring frequently.

3 Add chicken to skillet. Cook about 8 minutes, turning once, until brown. Add wine. Cook 8 to 10 minutes or until chicken is no longer pink in center. Serve with pasta.

1 Serving: Calories 275 (Calories from Fat 70); Total Fat 8g (Saturated Fat 2g); Cholesterol 85mg; Sodium 230mg; Carbohydrates 17g (Dietary Fiber 1g); Protein 34g

Bass with Parmesan

Prep Time: 10 min ■ Start to Finish: 25 min ■ 4 servings

1½ lb sea bass, sole or pike fillets
¼ cup all-purpose flour
2 tablespoons butter or margarine
2 medium green onions, thinly sliced (2 tablespoons)
1 cup dry white wine or chicken broth
2 tablespoons lemon juice
½ teaspoon salt
¼ teaspoon pepper
¼ cup freshly grated or shredded Parmesan cheese

1 Heat oven to 375°F. Coat fish fillets with flour; shake off excess flour. In 12-inch ovenproof skillet, melt butter over medium-low heat. Cook onions in butter about 5 minutes, stirring occasionally, until tender.

2 Add fish to skillet. Cook uncovered about 5 minutes or until light brown; carefully turn fish. Pour wine and lemon juice over fish. Sprinkle with salt, pepper and cheese.

3 Bake uncovered about 15 minutes or until cheese is melted and fish flakes easily with fork.

1 Serving: Calories 265 (Calories from Fat 90); Total Fat 10g (Saturated Fat 5g); Cholesterol 110mg; Sodium 590mg; Total Carbohydrate 8g (Fiber 0g); Protein 36g

Shrimp Scampi

Prep Time: 35 min ■ Start to Finish: 35 min ■ 6 servings

1½ lb uncooked medium shrimp in shells, thawed if frozen

2 tablespoons olive or vegetable oil

1 tablespoon chopped fresh parsley

2 tablespoons lemon juice

¼ teaspoon salt

2 medium green onions, thinly sliced (2 tablespoons)

2 cloves garlic, finely chopped

Grated Parmesan cheese, if desired

1 Peel shrimp. Make a shallow cut lengthwise down back of each shrimp; wash out vein.

2 In 10-inch skillet, heat oil over medium heat. Cook shrimp and remaining ingredients except cheese in oil 2 to 3 minutes, stirring frequently, until shrimp are pink; remove from heat. Sprinkle with cheese.

1 Serving: Calories 90 (Calories from Fat 35); Total Fat 4g (Saturated Fat 1g); Cholesterol 105mg; Sodium 220mg; Total Carbohydrate 1g (Dietary Fiber 0g); Protein 12g

Serve these succulent shrimp over a bed of hot fettuccine or angel hair pasta, and sprinkle with freshly chopped parsley.

Grilled Shrimp Kabobs with Fresh Herbs

Prep Time: 20 min ■ Start to Finish: 50 min ■ 6 servings

Rosemary-Lemon Marinade

12 six-inch-long sprigs rosemary

$1/4$ cup fresh lemon juice

3 tablespoons olive oil

1 tablespoon dry white wine or
    lemon juice

$1/2$ teaspoon salt

$1/2$ teaspoon pepper

Shrimp Kabobs

24 fresh large basil leaves

24 uncooked peeled deveined large
    shrimp (about $1 1/2$ pounds),
    with tails left on

12 small pattypan squash, cut in half

24 cherry tomatoes

24 large cloves garlic

1 Strip leaves from rosemary sprigs, leaving 1 inch of leaves at top intact; set sprigs aside for kabobs. Measure 1 tablespoon rosemary leaves; chop. (Store remaining leaves for other uses.) Mix chopped rosemary leaves and remaining marinaded ingredients. Wrap basil leaf around each shrimp.

2 For each kabob, thread shrimp, squash half, tomato and garlic clove alternately on stem of rosemary sprig, leaving space between each piece. (Start threading at stem end, pulling it through to leaves at top.) Place kabobs in ungreased rectangular baking dish, $13 \times 9 \times 2$ inches. Pour marinade over kabobs. Cover and refrigerate at least 20 minutes but no longer than 2 hours.

3 Brush grill rack with olive or vegetable oil. Heat coals or gas grill as directed by manufacturer for direct heat. Remove kabobs from marinade; reserve marinade. Cover and grill kabobs 5 to 6 inches from medium heat about 12 minutes, turning and brushing with marinade 2 or 3 times, until shrimp are pink and firm. Discard any remaining marinade.

1 Serving: Calories 105 (Calories from Fat 45); Fat 5g (Saturated 1g); Cholesterol 55mg; Sodium 200mg; Carbohydrate 9g (Dietary Fiber 2g); Protein 8g

Broiled Shrimp Kabobs with Fresh Herbs: Set oven control to broil. Spray rack of broiler pan with cooking spray, or brush with olive oil. Place kabobs on rack in broiler pan. Broil with tops about 4 inches from heat about 12 minutes, turning and brushing 2 or 3 times with marinade, until shrimp are pink and firm. Discard any remaining marinade.

Spicy Breaded Shrimp

Prep Time: 20 min ■ Start to Finish: 50 min ■ 6 servings

1½ lb uncooked medium shrimp in shells
2 eggs
3 tablespoons fresh lemon juice
3 tablespoons amaretto or ½ teaspoon almond extract
2 cloves garlic, finely chopped
Vegetable oil
¾ cup all-purpose flour
1 teaspoon salt
1 teaspoon ground red pepper (cayenne)
1 teaspoon ground cinnamon

1 Peel shrimp, leaving tails on. (If shrimp are frozen, do not thaw; peel in cold water.) Make a shallow cut lengthwise down back of each shrimp; wash out vein. Rinse shrimp; pat dry.

2 In large bowl, beat eggs slightly with fork. Stir in lemon juice, amaretto and garlic. Add shrimp; toss until shrimp are evenly coated. Cover and refrigerate 10 minutes.

3 In 4-quart Dutch oven, heat oil (2 to 3 inches) to 325°F. In small bowl, mix flour, salt, red pepper and cinnamon. Remove shrimp from bowl one at a time, and coat with flour mixture.

4 Fry 5 or 6 shrimp at a time about 2 minutes or until golden brown. Remove with slotted spoon. Drain on paper towels.

1 Serving: Calories 205 (Calories from Fat 100); Total Fat 11g (Saturated Fat 2g); Cholesterol 160mg; Sodium 430mg; Total Carbohydrate 13g (Dietary Fiber 1g); Protein 14g

Fresh Fruit Tart

Baked Raspberries with Brandy Sauce

Strawberries with Marsala Sauce

Panna Cotta

Almond Torte

Cannoli

Ricotta Cheesecake with Chocolate

Tiramisu

Chocolate Profiteroles

Anise Biscotti

Hazelnut Biscotti

Traditional Almond Cookies

Coffee and Chocolate Ice Cream

Neapolitan Ice Cream

Strawberry-Orange Ice

Lemon Ice

5 desserts

Fresh Fruit Tart

Prep Time: 10 min ▪ Start to Finish: 1 hr 5 min ▪ 8 servings

2 cups all-purpose flour

1 cup granulated sugar

$\frac{1}{2}$ cup butter or margarine, softened

1 teaspoon freshly grated lemon peel

1 teaspoon fresh lemon juice

1 teaspoon vanilla

3 eggs

$\frac{1}{2}$ cup apricot preserves

$\frac{1}{2}$ cup raspberry preserves

1 tablespoon amaretto or $\frac{1}{2}$ teaspoon almond extract

Fresh fruit topping (such as sliced apple, pear, banana, kiwifruit, figs, raspberries, blackberries, blueberries)

1 teaspoon honey

Powdered sugar, if desired

1 In medium bowl, mix flour, granulated sugar, butter, lemon peel, lemon juice, vanilla and eggs until dough forms. Place dough on lightly floured surface. Knead about 3 minutes or until dough holds together and is pliable. Shape dough into a ball. Cover with plastic wrap and refrigerate about 20 minutes or until firm.

2 Heat oven to 350°F. Butter and flour 11-inch round tart pan with removable bottom or 12-inch pizza pan. Pat dough evenly in pan. Bake about 35 minutes or until toothpick inserted in center comes out clean. Cool completely in pan on wire rack.

3 Heat apricot preserves and raspberry preserves until melted; stir in amaretto. Spread over crust. Arrange fresh fruit on top. Drizzle with honey; dust with powdered sugar. Serve immediately, or cover and refrigerate no longer than 1 hour.

1 Serving: Calories 495 (Calories from Fat 125); Total Fat 14g (Saturated Fat 8g); Cholesterol 110mg; Sodium 120mg; Total Carbohydrate 88g (Dietary Fiber 4g); Protein 7g

Baked Raspberries
with Brandy Sauce

Prep Time: 5 min ▪ Start to Finish: 25 min ▪ 8 servings

4 cups (2 pints) raspberries*
1¼ cups packed light brown sugar
½ cup brandy, amaretto or other liquor or liqueur
2 tablespoons honey
1 teaspoon vanilla
¼ cup butter or margarine, softened

1 Heat oven to 350°F. Place raspberries in ungreased 9-inch square baking dish. Mix remaining ingredients except butter until smooth; pour over raspberries. Dot with butter.

2 Bake uncovered about 20 minutes or until hot and bubbly. Stir gently, scraping bottom of dish to loosen sugar and stir into sauce. Serve warm.

*1½ bags (14- to 16-oz size) frozen loose-pack raspberries (without juice) can be substituted for the fresh raspberries. Rinse frozen berries with cold water to separate; continue as directed above.

1 Serving (about ½ cup each): Calories 240 (Calories from Fat 55); Total Fat 6g (Saturated Fat 4g); Cholesterol 15mg; Sodium 50mg; Total Carbohydrate 45g (Dietary Fiber 4g); Protein 1g

Strawberries with Marsala Sauce

Prep Time: 25 min ▪ Start to Finish: 35 min ▪ 6 servings

4 cups (2 pints) strawberries
2 cups sweet Marsala wine*
1/2 cup sugar
6 egg yolks

1 Remove stems from strawberries. Arrange strawberries, stem ends down, in shallow serving dish, about 10 inches in diameter. Pour 1 cup of the wine over strawberries.

2 Pour just enough water into bottom of double boiler so that top of double boiler does not touch water. Heat water over medium heat (do not boil).

3 Meanwhile, in top of double boiler, beat sugar and egg yolks using wire whisk, until pale yellow and slightly thickened. Place top of double boiler over bottom. Gradually beat remaining 1 cup wine into egg yolk mixture. Cook, beating constantly, until mixture thickens and coats whisk (do not boil).

4 Pour sauce over strawberries. Serve immediately.

*There is no substitute for sweet Marsala wine

1 Serving: Calories 250 (Calories from Fat 45); Fat 5g (Saturated 2g); Cholesterol 210mg; Sodium 15mg; Carbohydrate 33g (Dietary Fiber 2g); Protein 4g

Panna Cotta

Prep Time: 5 min ▪ Start to Finish: 4 hr 20 min ▪ 4 servings

2 cups half-and-half
1½ teaspoons unflavored gelatin
¼ cup sugar
1 teaspoon vanilla
Dash of salt

1 Pour half-and-half into 1½-quart saucepan. Sprinkle gelatin evenly over cold half-and-half. Let stand 10 minutes.

2 Heat half-and-half mixture over medium-high heat 5 to 7 minutes, stirring constantly, until gelatin is dissolved and mixture is just beginning to simmer (do not allow to boil). Remove from heat.

3 Stir in sugar, vanilla and salt until sugar is dissolved.

4 Pour mixture into four ½-cup ramekins or 6-oz custard cups. Cover with plastic wrap and refrigerate about 4 hours or until set.

5 When ready to serve, run thin knife around edge of each panna cotta. Dip bottom of each ramekin into bowl of very hot water for 5 seconds. Immediately place serving plate upside down onto each ramekin; turn plate and ramekin over and remove ramekin.

1 Serving: Calories 210 (Calories from Fat 130); Total Fat 14g (Saturated Fat 9g); Cholesterol 45mg; Sodium 125mg; Total Carbohydrate 18g (Dietary Fiber 0g); Protein 4g

Almond Torte

Prep Time: 15 min ▪ Start to Finish: 45 min ▪ 8 servings

1½ cups slivered almonds
2½ cups all-purpose flour
1 cup sugar
2 teaspoons baking powder
1 teaspoon salt
½ cup butter or margarine, softened
2 teaspoons almond extract
1 teaspoon vanilla
2 eggs
1 tablespoon sugar
Sliced strawberries, if desired
Sweetened whipped cream, if desired

1 Heat oven to 350°F. In ungreased shallow pan, spread almonds. Bake uncovered about 10 minutes, stirring occasionally, until golden brown; cool. Finely chop; set aside.

2 Grease 9-inch round cake pan. In medium bowl, mix flour, 1 cup sugar, the baking powder and salt. Stir in almonds, butter, almond extract, vanilla and eggs until stiff dough forms (dough will be slightly crumbly). Shape into 1-inch balls. Place in pan. Sprinkle with 1 tablespoon sugar.

3 Bake about 30 minutes or until golden brown. Cool on wire rack. Cut into wedges. Serve with strawberries and whipped cream.

1 Serving: Calories 490 (Calories from Fat 215); Total Fat 24g (Saturated Fat 9g); Cholesterol 85mg; Sodium 510mg; Total Carbohydrate 61g (Dietary Fiber 3g); Protein 10g

Cannoli

Prep time: 20 min ■ Start to Finish: 30 min ■ 12 pastries

½ cup slivered almonds
1 cup powdered sugar
1 container (15 oz) ricotta cheese
⅓ cup miniature semisweet chocolate chips
1 tablespoon amaretto or ⅛ teaspoon almond extract
12 cannoli pastry shells
12 maraschino cherries, cut in half
1 tablespoon powdered sugar
1 tablespoon baking cocoa

1 Heat oven to 350°F. Spread almonds in ungreased shallow pan. Bake uncovered about 10 minutes, stirring occasionally, until golden brown; cool.

2 In large bowl, gradually stir 1 cup powdered sugar into ricotta cheese. Stir in almonds, chocolate chips and amaretto.

3 Carefully spoon filling into pastry shells, filling from the center out. Place cherry half in filling on one end of each shell. In small bowl, mix 1 tablespoon powdered sugar and the cocoa; sprinkle over shells. Store covered in refrigerator.

1 Serving: Calories 270 (Calories from Fat 135); Total Fat 15g (Saturated Fat 4g); Cholesterol 10mg; Sodium 60mg; Total Carbohydrate 29g (Dietary Fiber 2g); Protein 7g

Ricotta Cheesecake with Chocolate

Prep Time: 15 min ▪ Start to Finish: 9 hr ▪ 8 servings

1 tablespoon sugar
1 tablespoon plain dry bread crumbs
1 container (15 oz) ricotta cheese
$1/2$ cup sugar
2 teaspoons grated lemon peel
4 egg yolks
$1/2$ cup all-purpose flour
$1/2$ cup finely chopped candied fruit
3 oz semisweet baking chocolate, grated or very finely chopped
2 egg whites
Sweetened whipped cream, if desired

1 Heat oven to 350°F. Grease 9-inch round cake pan. In small bowl, mix 1 tablespoon sugar and the bread crumbs. Coat bottom and side of pan with bread crumb mixture.

2 Drain any excess liquid from cheese. In medium bowl, mix cheese, $1/2$ cup sugar and the lemon peel. Stir in egg yolks, one at a time. Stir in flour, candied fruit and chocolate; set aside.

3 In medium bowl, beat egg whites with electric mixer on high speed until stiff. Fold cheese mixture into egg whites. Pour into pan.

4 Bake about 45 minutes or until set and edge is light brown. Refrigerate about 4 hours or until cool. Run knife or metal spatula around side of cheesecake to loosen; remove from pan. Cover and refrigerate at least 4 hours until chilled. Garnish with whipped cream. Store covered in refrigerator.

1 Serving: Calories 280 (Calories from Fat 90); Total Fat 10g (Saturated Fat 5g); Cholesterol 120mg; Sodium 125mg; Total Carbohydrate 39g (Dietary Fiber 1g); Protein 10g

Tiramisu

Prep Time: 1 hr ▪ Start to Finish: 6 hr ▪ 8 servings

6 egg yolks
¾ cup sugar
⅔ cup milk
1 lb mascarpone cheese or 2 packages (8 oz each) cream cheese, softened
1¼ cups heavy whipping cream
½ teaspoon vanilla
¼ cup brewed espresso or very strong coffee, chilled
2 tablespoons rum*
2 packages (3 oz each) ladyfingers
1 tablespoon baking cocoa

1 In 2-quart saucepan, beat egg yolks and sugar until well blended. Beat in milk. Heat to boiling over medium heat, stirring constantly; reduce heat to low. Boil and stir 1 minute; remove from heat. Pour into medium bowl; place plastic wrap directly onto surface of custard mixture. Refrigerate about 1 hour or until chilled.

2 Add cheese to custard mixture. Beat with electric mixer on medium speed until smooth; set aside. In chilled medium bowl, beat whipping cream and vanilla on high speed until stiff; set aside. Mix espresso and rum.

3 Separate ladyfingers horizontally; brush with espresso mixture (do not soak). In ungreased 11 × 7-inch baking dish, arrange half of the ladyfingers in single layer. Spread half of the cheese mixture over ladyfingers; spread with half of the whipped cream. Repeat layers with remaining ladyfingers, cheese mixture and whipped cream. Sprinkle with cocoa. Refrigerate at least 4 hours but no longer than 24 hours to develop flavors. Store covered in refrigerator.

*⅛ teaspoon rum extract mixed with 2 tablespoons water can be substituted for the rum.

1 Serving: Calories 535 (Calories from Fat 340); Total Fat 38g (Saturated Fat 22g); Cholesterol 270mg; Sodium 260mg; Total Carbohydrate 40g (Dietary Fiber 1g); Protein 9g

Chocolate Profiteroles

Prep Time: 30 min ▪ Start to Finish: 3 hr ▪ 6 servings

1 cup water
$\frac{1}{4}$ cup butter or margarine
$\frac{1}{2}$ teaspoon salt
1 cup all-purpose flour
4 eggs
1 cup heavy whipping cream
2 tablespoons powdered sugar
$\frac{1}{2}$ teaspoon freshly grated nutmeg
4 oz semisweet baking chocolate
2 tablespoons water
1 tablespoon honey

1 Heat oven to 400°F. Grease and flour cookie sheet.

2 In 2½-quart saucepan, heat 1 cup water, the butter and salt to rolling boil. Stir in flour. Stir vigorously over low heat about 1 minute or until mixture forms a ball. Remove from heat; cool 5 minutes. Beat in eggs, one at a time, until smooth. Drop by rounded tablespoonfuls about 2 inches apart onto cookie sheet.

3 Bake about 30 minutes or until puffed and golden brown. Remove from cookie sheet to wire rack; cool. Cut off tops of puffs; reserve. Pull out any filaments of soft dough from puffs.

4 In chilled medium bowl, beat whipping cream, powdered sugar and nutmeg with electric mixer on high speed until stiff. Fill puffs with whipped cream mixture; replace tops. Mound puffs on large serving plate.

5 In 2-quart saucepan, heat remaining ingredients over low heat until smooth; drizzle over puffs. Freeze at least 2 hours until chocolate is firm, or serve immediately. Store covered in refrigerator.

1 Serving: Calories 425 (Calories from Fat 260); Total Fat 29g (Saturated Fat 17g); Cholesterol 205mg; Sodium 310mg; Total Carbohydrate 35g (Dietary Fiber 2g); Protein 8g

Anise Biscotti

Prep: 15 min ▪ Start to Finish: 1 hr 5 min ▪ About 42 cookies

1 cup sugar
1/2 cup butter or margarine, softened
2 teaspoons anise seed, ground
2 teaspoons grated lemon peel
2 eggs
3 1/2 cups all-purpose flour
1 teaspoon baking powder
1/2 teaspoon salt

1 Heat oven to 350°F. In large bowl, beat sugar, butter, anise, lemon peel and eggs. Stir in flour, baking powder and salt.

2 Divide dough in half. Shape half of dough into 10 × 3-inch rectangle, rounding edges slightly, on one end of ungreased cookie sheet. Repeat with remaining dough on same cookie sheet.

3 Bake about 25 minutes or until center is firm to the touch. Cool on cookie sheet 15 minutes; move to cutting board. Cut each rectangle crosswise into 1/2-inch slices, using sharp knife.

4 Place slices, cut sides down, on ungreased cookie sheet. Bake about 15 minutes or until crisp and light brown. Immediately remove from cookie sheet to cooling rack; cool.

1 Cookie: Calories 85 (Calories from Fat 25); Total Fat 3g (Saturated Fat 1g); Cholesterol 15mg; Sodium 55mg; Total Carbohydrate 13g (Dietary Fiber 0g); Protein 1g

Hazelnut Biscotti

Prep Time: 25 min ▪ Start to Finish: 1 hr 20 min ▪ About 42 cookies

1 cup hazelnuts (filberts), coarsely chopped
1 cup sugar
1/2 cup butter or margarine, softened
1 teaspoon almond extract
1 teaspoon vanilla
2 eggs
3 1/2 cups all-purpose flour
1 teaspoon baking powder
1/2 teaspoon baking soda

1 Heat oven to 350°F. Spread hazelnuts in ungreased shallow pan. Bake uncovered about 10 minutes, stirring occasionally, until golden brown; cool.

2 In large bowl, beat sugar, butter, almond extract, vanilla and eggs. Stir in flour, baking powder and baking soda. Stir in hazelnuts. Place dough on lightly floured surface. Gently knead 2 to 3 minutes or until dough holds together and hazelnuts are evenly distributed.

3 Divide dough in half. Shape half of dough into 10 × 3-inch rectangle, rounding edges slightly, on one side of ungreased cookie sheet. Repeat with remaining dough on same cookie sheet.

4 Bake about 25 minutes or until center is firm to the touch. Cool on cookie sheet 15 minutes; move to cutting board. Cut each rectangle crosswise into 1/2-inch slices, using sharp knife.

5 Place slices, cut sides down, on ungreased cookie sheet. Bake about 15 minutes or until crisp and light brown. Immediately remove from cookie sheet to cooling rack; cool.

1 Cookie: Calories 95 (Calories from Fat 35); Total Fat 4g (Saturated Fat 2g); Cholesterol 15mg; Sodium 45mg; Total Carbohydrate 13g (Dietary Fiber 0g); Protein 2g

Traditional Almond Cookies

Prep Time: 20 min ▪ Start to Finish: 45 min ▪ About 48 cookies

3 cups slivered almonds
3 jumbo egg whites
1½ cups granulated sugar
1 teaspoon powdered sugar
1 teaspoon amaretto or ¼ teaspoon almond extract
Granulated sugar

1 Heat oven to 350°F. Spread almonds in ungreased shallow pan. Bake uncovered about 10 minutes, stirring occasionally, until golden brown; cool.

2 Reduce oven temperature to 300°F. Line cookie sheet with cooking parchment paper, or grease and flour cookie sheet.

3 Place almonds in food processor or blender. Cover and process until finely ground but not paste-like.

4 In medium bowl, beat egg whites with electric mixer on high speed until stiff. Stir in almonds, 1½ cups granulated sugar, the powdered sugar and amaretto. Drop by rounded teaspoonfuls about 2 inches apart onto cookie sheet. Sprinkle with granulated sugar.

5 Bake 20 to 25 minutes or until light golden brown. Cool 5 minutes. Remove from cookie sheet to cooling rack; cool.

1 Cookie: Calories 75 (Calories from Fat 35); Total Fat 4g (Saturated Fat 0g); Cholesterol 0mg; Sodium 5mg; Total Carbohydrate 9g (Dietary Fiber 1g); Protein 2g

Coffee and Chocolate Ice Cream

Prep Time: 20 min ▪ Start to Finish: 2 hr 30 min ▪ 8 servings

¾ cup sugar
1 cup whole milk
1 tablespoon freeze-dried instant coffee (dry)
1 teaspoon baking cocoa
2 eggs
1 cup heavy whipping cream

1 In 2-quart saucepan, mix all ingredients except whipping cream. Cook over medium heat, stirring constantly, 5 or 6 minutes or until mixture reaches 165°F. Cover and refrigerate about 1 hour 30 minutes or until cool.

2 In chilled medium bowl, beat whipping cream with electric mixer on high speed until soft peaks form. Fold milk mixture into whipped cream. Freeze in ice-cream maker as directed by manufacturer.

1 Serving (½ cup each): Calories 215 (Calories from Fat 110); Total Fat 12g (Saturated Fat 7g); Cholesterol 90mg; Sodium 40mg; Total Carbohydrate 21g (Dietary Fiber 0g); Protein 3g

Neapolitan Ice Cream

Prep Time: 25 min ■ Start to Finish: 2 hr 25 min ■ 7 servings

1 cup milk
³/₄ cup sugar
4 egg yolks
¹/₂ cup hazelnuts (filberts)
1 cup heavy whipping cream
¹/₂ teaspoon baking cocoa

1 In 2-quart saucepan, mix milk, sugar and egg yolks. Cook over medium heat, stirring constantly, 5 or 6 minutes or until mixture reaches 165°F. Cover and refrigerate about 1 hour 30 minutes or until cool.

2 Heat oven to 400°F. Spread hazelnuts in ungreased shallow pan. Bake uncovered about 5 minutes or until skins begin to crack. Wrap hazelnuts in clean towel; let stand 2 minutes. Rub hazelnuts in towel to remove skins. Finely chop hazelnuts; return to pan. Bake about 8 minutes, stirring occasionally, until golden brown; cool.

3 In chilled medium bowl, beat whipping cream with electric mixer on high speed until soft peaks form. Fold milk mixture, hazelnuts and cocoa into whipped cream. Freeze in ice-cream maker as directed by manufacturer.

1 Serving (¹/₂ cup each): Calories 510 (Calories from Fat 305); Total Fat 34g (Saturated 17g); Cholesterol 300mg; Sodium 60mg; Total Carbohydrate 45g (Dietary Fiber 1g); Protein 8g

Strawberry-Orange Ice

Prep Time: 15 min ▪ Start to Finish: 3 hr 25 min ▪ 8 servings

2 cups water
1/3 cup sugar
1/2 cup fresh orange juice
12 very ripe strawberries, mashed well (1/2 cup)
1 teaspoon vanilla

1 In 2-quart saucepan, heat water to boiling. Stir in remaining ingredients except vanilla. Boil 3 minutes, stirring constantly. Remove from heat; stir in vanilla. Cool 10 minutes.

2 Freeze in ice-cream maker as directed by manufacturer. Or cool to room temperature, then pour into ungreased 9 × 5-inch loaf pan, and freeze 1 hour 30 minutes to 2 hours or until mushy in center. Stir mixture; freeze about 1 hour longer, stirring every 30 minutes, until firm. Stir again before serving.

3 Serve in chilled dessert dishes. Or cut into 1/2-inch chunks and place in serving bowl. Cover and freeze until ready to serve.

1 Serving (1/2 cup each): Calories 45 (Calories from Fat 0); Total Fat 0g (Saturated 0g); Cholesterol 0mg; Sodium 0mg; Total Carbohydrate 11g (Dietary Fiber 0g); Protein 0g

Procopio Coltelli, a Sicilian, was a master at making ice cream and ices. In the eighteenth century, he opened an ice-cream parlor in Paris—Europe's first—and popularized Italian ices. His store was a tradition for roughly two hundred years, passed down through generations of the Coltelli family.

Lemon Ice

Prep Time: 20 min ▪ Start to Finish: 1 hr 10 min ▪ 8 servings

2 cups water
1 cup sugar
1 tablespoon grated lemon peel
1 cup fresh lemon juice

1 In 2-quart saucepan, heat water and sugar to boiling; reduce heat. Simmer uncovered 5 minutes; remove from heat. Stir in lemon peel and lemon juice. Cool 10 minutes.

2 Freeze in ice-cream maker as directed by manufacturer. Or cool to room temperature, then pour into ungreased 9 × 5-inch loaf pan, and freeze 1 hour 30 minutes to 2 hours or until mushy in center. Stir mixture; freeze about 1 hour longer, stirring every 30 minutes, until firm. Stir again before serving.

3 Serve in chilled dessert dishes. Or cut into ½-inch chunks and place in serving bowl. Cover and freeze until ready to serve.

1 Serving (½ cup each): Calories 110 (Calories from Fat 0); Total Fat 0g (Saturated Fat 0g); Cholesterol 0mg; Sodium 5mg; Total Carbohydrate 27g (Dietary Fiber 0g); Protein 0g

Cool down on a hot, steamy day with this beautiful frosty dessert. For an elegant presentation, hollow out fresh lemon halves, and trim a thin slice off the bottom of each half so lemons stand flat. Pile them high with luscious lemon ice, and keep them in the freezer until ready to serve. Fill stemmed wineglasses with crushed ice. Nestle a lemon half in the ice, and add fragrant fresh mint or lemon geranium leaves for the finishing touch.

Helpful Nutrition and Cooking Information

Recommended intake for a daily diet of 2,000 calories as set by the Food and Drug Administration

Total Fat	Less than 65g
Saturated Fat	Less than 20g
Cholesterol	Less than 300mg
Sodium	Less than 2,400mg
Total Carbohydrate	300g
Dietary Fiber	25g

Calculating Nutrition Information

- The first ingredient was used wherever a choice is given (such as $1/3$ cup sour cream or plain yogurt).

- The first ingredient amount was used wherever a range is given (such as 3- to $3^1/_2$-pound cut-up broiler-fryer chicken).

- The first serving number was used wherever a range is given (such as 4 to 6 servings).

- "If desired" ingredients and recipe variations were not included (such as sprinkle with brown sugar, if desired).

- Only the amount of a marinade or frying oil that is estimated to be absorbed by the food during preparation or cooking was calculated.

Ingredients Used in Recipe Testing and Nutrition Calculations

- Ingredients used for testing represent those that the majority of consumers use in their homes: large eggs, 2% milk, 80%-lean ground beef, canned ready-to-use chicken broth and vegetable oil spread containing not less than 65% fat.

- Fat-free, low-fat or low-sodium products were not used, unless otherwise indicated.

- Solid vegetable shortening (not butter, margarine, nonstick cooking sprays or vegetable oil spread as they can cause sticking problems) was used to grease pans, unless otherwise indicated.

Equipment Used in Recipe Testing

We use equipment for testing that the majority of consumers use in their homes. If a specific piece of equipment (such as a whisk) is necessary for recipe success, it is listed in the recipe.

- Cookware and bakeware without nonstick coatings were used, unless otherwise indicated.

- No dark-colored, black or insulated bakeware was used.

- When a pan is specified in a recipe, a metal pan was used; a baking dish or pie plate means ovenproof glass was used.

- An electric hand mixer was used for mixing only when mixer speeds are specified in the recipe directions. When a mixer speed is not given, a spoon or fork was used.

Metric Conversion Guide

VOLUME

U.S. Units	Canadian Metric	Australian Metric
¹/₄ teaspoon	1 mL	1 ml
¹/₂ teaspoon	2 mL	2 ml
1 teaspoon	5 mL	5 ml
1 tablespoon	15 mL	20 ml
¹/₄ cup	50 mL	60 ml
¹/₃ cup	75 mL	80 ml
¹/₂ cup	125 mL	125 ml
²/₃ cup	150 mL	170 ml
³/₄ cup	175 mL	190 ml
1 cup	250 mL	250 ml
1 quart	1 liter	1 liter
1¹/₂ quarts	1.5 liters	1.5 liters
2 quarts	2 liters	2 liters
2¹/₂ quarts	2.5 liters	2.5 liters
3 quarts	3 liters	3 liters
4 quarts	4 liters	4 liters

WEIGHT

U.S. Units	Canadian Metric	Australian Metric
1 ounce	30 grams	30 grams
2 ounces	55 grams	60 grams
3 ounces	85 grams	90 grams
4 ounces (¹/₄ pound)	115 grams	125 grams
8 ounces (¹/₂ pound)	225 grams	225 grams
16 ounces (1 pound)	455 grams	500 grams
1 pound	455 grams	0.5 kilogram

MEASUREMENTS

Inches	Centimeters
1	2.5
2	5.0
3	7.5
4	10.0
5	12.5
6	15.0
7	17.5
8	20.5
9	23.0
10	25.5
11	28.0
12	30.5
13	33.0

TEMPERATURES

Fahrenheit	Celsius
32°	0°
212°	100°
250°	120°
275°	140°
300°	150°
325°	160°
350°	180°
375°	190°
400°	200°
425°	220°
450°	230°
475°	240°
500°	260°

NOTE: The recipes in this cookbook have not been developed or tested using metric measures. When converting recipes to metric, some variations in quality may be noted.

Index

Page numbers in *italics* indicate illustrations.